Greenhouse Gardening For a Sustainable Future

An Eco-Friendly Guide to Growing Organic Fruits and Vegetables Year Round

Kacey Collier

© Copyright Kimberly Collier 2022 - All rights reserved.

The content contained within this book may not be reproduced, duplicated, or transmitted without direct written permission from the author or the publisher.

Under no circumstances will any blame or legal responsibility be held against the publisher, or author, for any damages, reparation, or monetary loss due to the information contained within this book. Either directly or indirectly. You are responsible for your own choices, actions, and results.

Legal Notice:

This book is copyright protected. This book is only for personal use. You cannot amend, distribute, sell, use, quote or paraphrase any part, or the content within this book, without the consent of the author or publisher.

Disclaimer Notice:

Please note the information contained within this document is for educational and entertainment purposes only. All effort has been executed to present accurate, up-to-date, and reliable, complete information. No warranties of any kind are declared or implied. Readers acknowledge that the author is not rendering legal, financial, medical or professional advice. The content within this book has been derived from various sources. Please consult a licensed professional before attempting any techniques outlined in this book.

By reading this document, the reader agrees that under no circumstances is the author responsible for any losses, direct or indirect, which are incurred as a result of the use of the information contained within this document, including, but not limited to, — errors, omissions, or inaccuracies.

Dedication

This book is dedicated to my coach Tony Scott. You were gone before we even got started. But what you taught me during that short time was incredible. Rest in Peace.

This book is also dedicated to my grandmother Beatrice James. She grew a peach tree from a pit in the middle of Chicago. I love and miss her garden. Peonies will forever be my favorite flower. Thank You Grandma for all that you taught me. I hope this book make you proud!

Contents

Introduction	1
1. The Right Greenhouse for You	7
The Structural Styles of a Greenhouse	
Choosing Materials for Your Greenhouse	
Building with Unconventional Materials	
Greenhouse Location and Size	
Essential Systems for Every Greenhouse	
Essential Tools for the Greenhouse	
How Much Does It Cost?	
The Takeaway	
Take Action	
2. How to Use Every Inch of Your Greenhouse for Plants	40
Greenhouse Staging	
Material Types	
The Benefits of Raised Bed Gardening	
Container Growing	
Going Vertical	

     Ideal Plants for Vertical Gardening
     The Takeaway
     Take Action

3. From Seed to Table: How to Grow and Enjoy Fresh Fruits and Vegetables   56
     The Best Fruits and Vegetables to Plant in your Greenhouse
     Planting Seeds
     Transplanting Seedlings from the Tray
     Watering Your Seedlings
     Taking Care of Growing Plants
     When to Harvest Your Fruits and Vegetables
     The Takeaway
     Your Plan

4. Using Sustainable Gardening Strategies to Grow More Food.   77
     Square-Foot Gardening
     Crop Rotation
     Hydroponics
     Succession Planning
     The Takeaway
     Take Action

5. Companion Planting for a Bountiful Greenhouse Harvest   93
     Why Companion Planting Works
     Best Companion Plants for Your Vegetables

     Best Companion Plants for Your Fruits
     Flavor and Scent with Companion Herbs and Spices

      Flowers for Your Food and Food for Pollinators
      The Takeaway
      Take Action

6. The Dark Side: Soil Health in Greenhouse   109
      Why Is Soil Health Important?
      Understanding your Soil
      Soil Amendments
      Takeaway
      Take Action

7. Pest, Disease, and Sanitation Management for   126
   Greenhouse Gardeners
      Pest Control the Natural Way

      Identifying and Treating Common Pests
      The Dangers of Fungus, Bacterial Diseases, and Viruses
      Organic Fungicides and Prevention: Alternative Homemade Anti-fungal Solutions
      Bacterial Control and Prevention
      Viruses
      Sanitation for Greenhouses
      Cleaning Your Greenhouse
      Tips on Cleaning Your Gardening Tools
      Take Away
      Take Action

8. Greenhouse Gardening In Every Season   153
      Greenhouse Gardening in the Spring
      Greenhouse Gardening in the Summer
      Greenhouse Gardening in the Fall
      Greenhouse Gardening in the Winter

The Takeaway
Conclusion   161

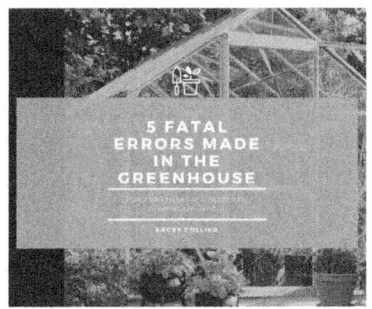

Download your Free Gift

Learn how to recognize and avoid the most common mistakes made in the greenhouse

Discover innovative solutions for preventing costly errors

Equip yourself with the knowledge to optimize your greenhouses' performance and yield potential!

https://bit.ly/greenhousemistakes

Introduction

How clean and safe do you think your food is?

I'm not sure about you, but every time I pop a strawberry in my mouth, I wonder how many pesticides are hiding within those nooks and crannies.

Of course, I wash them as thoroughly as possible but knowing that they grow being sprayed with all sorts of chemicals has never given me much reassurance.

I used to think I was being paranoid. That is until I discovered that strawberries are some of the most pesticide-laden fruits in the grocery store. With their bright red color and intoxicating aroma, these delicious strawberries were excellent for my health. Strawberries are naturally chock full of great vitamins and antioxidants. However, to my dismay, strawberries and many fruits and vegetables we consider vital to good health are sprayed with pesticides from the beginning. If you're like me and are just discovering these things, then you're not alone.

> *"The food you eat can be either the safest and most powerful form of medicine or the slowest form of poison."*
>
> *– Ann Wigmore.*

I don't know about you, but not only do I want a long life, but I also want a healthy life. And I worry. I worry about what is happening in this world and what we are doing to our earth. Long before the Covid-19 pandemic, I was concerned about the impact of how we live on the planet. But Covid-19 brought it into complete focus. I assumed I could always go to the store and buy food if I had money. For the first time in my life, I looked at empty grocery store shelves. My brother had to ask our family around the country to look for baby formula because it was in short supply. I know I'm not alone in the feeling of despair and wondering what I could do. I never want to feel as if I will not have access to food. And the idea of storing hundreds of canned goods in case of another pandemic makes me sick to my stomach. So, I learned how to grow my own food.

GREENHOUSE GARDENING FOR A SUSTAINABLE FU...

The more I investigated the farming industry, the more I knew I wanted to do something different. From the impact of poor farming practices on our land and waterways to the quality of fruit when it's flown in from across the world, we are doing something wrong. I decided to do my part to take care of this earth because it is my home. Plus, I like a challenge. I wrote this book for all the people like me looking for ways to be a better steward of the earth and enjoy the connection of growing plants of all kinds. If you never want to stand helpless in the grocery store wondering if there will be any food for you, then read

his book is a collection of my experiences and research on the best ways to grow food year-round. I choose greenhouse gardening because I live in Chicago, the Windy City. If you know anything about my city, you know the summers are hot, and the winters are COLD! I was skeptical that anything could grow during our cold winter months. But I discovered that many cold-tolerant vegetables taste better because of the old. I also learned that a greenhouse, even an unheated greenhouse, can give you the edge you need to grow vegetables all year long.

I also did a lot of research on eco-friendly gardening practices. Like you, I battled pests in my garden. Nothing was more disappointing than seeing my lettuce beautiful one day but covered with white flies the next. I even found a caterpillar happily munching away in my herb garden. I named him Petey. I went to my local garden center but was confused about the available pesticides. I read one label that said it was dangerous to beneficial insects like bees. I was appalled. I just let Petey and the white flies have it. I didn't want to kill the bees. I wanted to find a better way to have a garden without pests or nasty pesticides. Fortunately, there are many ways to protect your garden from unwanted pests WITHOUT killing bees and butterflies. Using some of the eco-friendly gardening practices in this book can protect your garden from pests and increase your harvest.

This book is for anyone who wants to learn about greenhouse gardening and how to make it sustainable. It is perfect for beginners who want to start their own greenhouse garden and experienced gardeners who want to add to their knowledge.

In this book, you will learn:

- How to select the right greenhouse for your needs
- How to maximize the space in your greenhouse so you can grow more food.
- How to nurture plants from seed to harvest.
- Eco-friendly gardening practices that protect and increase your harvest
- How to keep your greenhouse clean and your plants healthy

But most importantly, you will learn how to grow fruits and vegetables all year long.

GREENHOUSE GARDENING FOR A SUSTAINABLE FU...

With these tips and tricks, you can start or expand your greenhouse gardening journey and play a part in creating a sustainable future for our planet.

Thanks,

Kacey Collier

CHAPTER 1

THE RIGHT GREENHOUSE FOR YOU

We begin this greenhouse journey with two goals. First, to build a greenhouse good for the earth and second, to grow food good for the body. Accomplishing both goals may seem daunting. But with thought and planning, you can achieve both.

When building a greenhouse, there are a few things to remember if you want it to be environmentally friendly. First, consider the structures and materials used in building your greenhouse. Look for structures made from recycled materials. Use renewable energy options like solar panels. The location of your greenhouse also matters - try to orient it so it takes advantage of sunlight and uses insulating materials to maintain steady temperatures inside. In addition, think about how you can utilize ventilation instead of relying on artificial heating and cooling. With tools and resources such as water, prioritize those that are sustainable and low impact. Considering all these factors, you can have an eco-friendly greenhouse that supports your plants and the planet.

This chapter will discuss the pros and cons of different types of greenhouses to help you decide the best one for you. We will also cover the ideal location for a greenhouse and the systems for plants to grow in a greenhouse, such as light, heat, ventilation, and water. We will finish with the basic tools you need in a greenhouse.

The Structural Styles of a Greenhouse

The design of your greenhouse is essential so you can maximize sunlight and save energy. Modular construction, or prefabricated construction, saves time, money, and energy during the construction process. If you have construction knowledge, then there is no stopping you from creating your own design and saving even more money. However, whether you design your greenhouse or use a pre-fabricated structure, you must determine the structural style of the greenhouse. This section will explore the typical structural styles that can work in most backyards.

Lean-To-Greenhouse

A lean-to greenhouse is named after the greenhouse's structure. This type of greenhouse is attached to the outside wall of a home or building. A lean-to greenhouse typically has two to three sides that allow light to enter the structure, including the roof. The final side is the wall of a pre-existing home or building.

Most lean-to greenhouses have a limited amount of gardening space available. Typically a gardener could place plants on either side of the greenhouse. However, in a lean-to greenhouse, shelf space is limited because only one side of the garden is available for plants. Gardeners overcome this limitation by extending the length of their greenhouse to provide more space.

- **Advantages-** Lean-to greenhouses have lower costs because the roof requires less structural support. You can easily set up this greenhouse in a small space, and because it leans against an existing structure, water and electricity are easily accessible.

- **Disadvantages-** You will have a limited area, with fewer plants to grow. It will be harder to control airflow, temperature, and sunlight. The lean-to will largely depend on the wall structure to which it is attached.

Even-span Greenhouse

An even-span greenhouse is identifiable by its two roofs, which slope equally in terms of angle and size. This is easily the most popular design whenever anyone thinks about a greenhouse.

Compared to other greenhouse structures, an even-span greenhouse will cost less to construct and provide lots of garden space. All sides of the even-span greenhouse have glass panels or similar material that allows sunlight to pass through. They are visually pleasing, and if you get a pre-fabricated model, there are many options from which to choose.

- **Advantages-** The flexible and spacious designs allow a range of sizes for setup. The structure promotes ease in maintaining temperature and airflow. It discourages snow and water from accumulating on the structure. This design allows more space to grow plants while still moving freely.

- **Disadvantages-** Depending on materials, even-span greenhouses can be more costly to construct and usually require a heating system.

Poly-Tunnel or Hoop House

A poly-tunnel greenhouse is an excellent option for those who want to garden but don't have the space or resources for a traditional greenhouse. Poly-tunnels are relatively inexpensive and can be easily assembled, making them a popular choice for gardeners of all levels of experience. They work by using hoops made from metal or plastic covered in a layer of fabric. This insulating fabric traps heat within its fibers, creating an optimal growth climate for plants. . Poly-tunnels can grow various plants, including vegetables, fruits, and flowers.

- **Advantages**- They're relatively inexpensive. This is especially true if you build the greenhouse yourself. They're easy to construct. With even the most basic carpentry skills, you can assemble a poly-tunnel greenhouse in an instant and be ready to start growing plants by the end of the weekend. There are plenty of plans and kits available online.

- **Disadvantages**- They're not as attractive as traditional glass greenhouses. A poly-tunnel greenhouse is probably not the best choice if looks are important to you. They're not as durable as traditional glass greenhouses. Despite their robust construction, the cover of a poly-tunnel will need to be replaced every 4-5 years.

Gothic Arch Greenhouse

This style of greenhouse features curved wall structures bent over the frame. The design eventually leads toward a pointed roof while eliminating the need for trusses. The lack of trusses requires fewer materials and reduced labor. The unique shape also allows snow and water to run off the structure quickly.

This design type can be adapted to small spaces or large commercial farms.

- **Advantages-** The design is versatile enough for small- to large-scale structures. The distinctive shape holds a high aesthetic value for many people. It does not require trusses, reducing costs. Snow and water easily slide off this type of greenhouse.

- **Disadvantages-** The gothic arch greenhouse can be challenging to build compared to other designs. The structure can have reduced ventilation due to its lower headroom. Overall costs can eventually turn out higher than different types.

Choosing Materials for Your Greenhouse

When building an eco-friendly greenhouse, every aspect counts. Know that every material has advantages and disadvantages, even materials that seem eco-friendly. A biodegradable material like wood may not be as strong or long-lasting as steel. You may live in an area with intense weather. It may be more eco-friendly to go with steel for strength and durability. Being mindful in every step of construction can make a massive difference in creating a more environmentally friendly greenhouse.

Understanding the Basic Greenhouse Structure

A greenhouse is typically made of a translucent material (typically glass) attached to a frame. The translucent material allows the light to pass through to the plants. Translucent materials can be anything from glass and fiberglass to plastic sheeting. This material is laid against a frame that creates the building. The frame is like the skeleton of a body. It consists of the side walls, end walls, side posts, rafters, and horizontal beams to the rafters called purlins. Most people prefer to use metal frames for sturdiness and freedom of movement. Yet greenhouse structures can be made of many types of materials. Understanding the different kinds of framing materials available will affect the durability and sustainability of the entire structure.

The Frame

Frames can be made from many materials, including wood, galvanized steel, aluminum, and even plastic. Considering the frame in relation to the size and locations of the structure you are building is essential. Plastic is an easy frame for smaller greenhouses protected from the elements. However, it is not environmentally friendly. Galvanized steel provides strength to a greenhouse subjected to many storms. Wood may be a less expensive option for an area that does not experience extensive rainfall.

- **Wood**- A wood frame is more affordable and environmentally friendly but can deteriorate quickly. This material is suitable for areas with more temperate weather and little rain.

- **Galvanized Steel**- Galvanized steel is durable and can withstand more extreme weather. However, the galvanizing process for steel is questionable on its environmental impact.

- **Aluminum**- Aluminum is lightweight and durable. It is also 100% recyclable. But it is a more expensive material.

- **Plastic**- Plastic is lightweight, durable, and affordable but can be flammable, difficult to insure, and not environmentally friendly. Use this material with caution. Avoid it if possible.

The Cover

Determining the translucent materials to cover your frame is a critical decision. It is vital because your choice will affect the light your plants receive. Popular greenhouse coverings include glass, polycarbonate, acrylic, fiberglass, double-sheet polyethylene films, and PVC-based materials. As always, you must measure benefits against the cost to your pocket and the environment.

Glass

This is one of the oldest and most popular greenhouse coverings, thanks to its beautiful appearance. Fortunately, glass is sustainable and recyclable. However, glass can be costly to build, heat, and protect from the elements.

There are two main styles of glass greenhouses to consider.

- **Single Pane-** This is ideal for warmer climates but can be more fragile and allow heat to escape.
- **Double Pane-** This is ideal for cooler regions and retains heat better but can cost more if coated with special treatments.

Polycarbonate

Greenhouses with polycarbonate coverings are lower in cost than glass. The thick plastic opaque material is superior to glass. It is also recyclable. However, polycarbonate has its own issues, such as clouding and yellowing.

Like glass panels, polycarbonate panels come in two types.

- **Single-wall-** Single-wall polycarbonate is durable but does not insulate heat or diffuse light. It can be flammable and hard to insure.
- **Twin-wall-** Twin-wall polycarbonate is durable and diffuses light better but can retain condensation that may cause plant disease.

Polyethylene Film

Polyethylene films are lightweight and inexpensive, making them very convenient. This porous material allows carbon dioxide and oxygen to pass through greenhouses, allowing plants to breathe. It, too, is recyclable. This type of covering is typically used with hoop houses.

This material is popular among gardeners because it can be easily customized by applying different coatings. Some coatings reduce sun damage, prevent condensation, and even diffuse light. However, despite their versatility, polyethylene films are flammable and may not be easily insured.

Fiberglass

Fiberglass is another option to cover your greenhouse. The material provides light diffusion and transmission and can last up to a decade. It, however, is not recyclable so use it with caution. UV rays can break down the material over time, so you may need to apply a UV protection coat to strengthen it every few years. If you prefer fiberglass, then look for a greenhouse being sold. If you reuse the materials, you keep them out of the landfill.

PVC Fabric

PVC fabric is one of the best choices for cooler climates with durability because it provides increased insulation while withstanding heavy snow. PVC fabrics can have UV stabilizers that prevent yellowing and damage from the sun. The fabric can be coated to be flame-retardant. Additionally, PVC fabrics are easy to install, allowing you to build your greenhouse easily and quickly. However, PVC is a material you should avoid if you can. Only a particular type of PVC material is recyclable. Further, if PVC of any kind is left in a landfill, it will leach dangerous toxins into the earth around it.

Opaque vs. Clear Panels

When I started on my greenhouse journey, I assumed that the paneling in a greenhouse had to be clear. Clear paneling lets in the most light, and I thought that's what plants need. But that is not necessarily true. Clear panels are best for germinating seeds to produce seedlings for outside transplants. The light from the sun warms the soil, which stimulates seed germination. Clear panels also allow more heat into your greenhouse. If you're located in a region that experiences harsh weather conditions during winter or summer, it is essential to consider the optimal heating solutions for your greenhouse. The benefit of opaque panels is that they create more diffused light in your greenhouse. Diffused light is better for plants grown to maturity as it provides lighting and avoids hot spots. Diffused light allows for more efficient photosynthesis and more compact plant growth.

Pro Tip

- Use white or light-colored materials for the rest of your greenhouse to increase diffused and reflected light.

The Flooring

Before I had a greenhouse, I never thought flooring had such a significant impact on the overall functioning of the greenhouse. Not only should it provide a stable, level surface for you and your plants, but it must also deal effectively with water and dirt. Flooring can affect the heating and cooling of your greenhouse and can even affect the health of your plants.

There are many greenhouse flooring options, from mulch to porous concrete. Porous concrete is popular. It is easy to clean and can be poured so it drains water, retains heat, and reflects sunlight. It is a powerful barrier to weeds and pests that live in the dirt and will last a long time. Concrete is considered a recyclable, sustainable material. However, it can be less comfortable to stand and walk on as compared to other options and may be more expensive.

On the flip side, mulch is a great solution. Mulch is inexpensive and drains water well. Mulch is also eco-friendly. However, mulch breaks down quickly and can be a hassle to replace. It also allows pests and weeds easy access to your greenhouse.

For those who are not yet prepared to commit to concrete, there are numerous other sustainable flooring options available.

- **Lava and Landscape Rocks** come in many colors allowing you to increase the visual appeal of your greenhouse. They soak up water and release it into the air, thus improving humidity. When using lava and landscape rocks, remember to use a weed cloth underneath. Drawbacks include the expense and difficulty of cleaning the stones.

- **Bricks on sand and clay floors** are long-lasting and are more comfortable than concrete. Bricks increase the humidity in a greenhouse. It also traps and releases water back into the air. Both flooring materials cost about the same as a concrete floor.

- **Gravel floors** are inexpensive and provide good drainage but must be used with weed cloth. It is also easy to install and requires little maintenance.

- **Vinyl floors** are increasing in popularity. They are durable and easy to maintain. They may be laid as a path or used over the entire floor to add visual appeal. They can also be treated to be UV-resistant, anti-bacterial, and anti-microbial. However, vinyl is not biodegradable and must be recycled.

Another approach to flooring is to consider using the earth. Many gardeners prefer to grow plants straight into the ground. Growing your plant directly into the ground is called a direct sow. You'd choose your ideal growing site and construct your greenhouse around your selected patch of ground.

Pro Tip

- Consider how much traffic your greenhouse will see. If you're only using it occasionally, you won't need to worry about choosing a super durable flooring material. However, if you're planning on using your greenhouse daily, you'll want to select a material that can withstand a lot of foot traffic, like concrete or stone.

Building with Unconventional Materials

While I have given details on the conventional materials used to construct greenhouses, you don't need to be limited by those options. After all, a greenhouse can virtually be built from anything: take advantage of this fact and let your creativity shine! Invest your time and energy in finding recyclable materials for your greenhouse to reduce your carbon impact on this earth. Some materials I will suggest may surprise you. But I love that you can create a greenhouse that is original and has character, all while recycling materials. Finding and recycling materials also decrease the impact on your pocketbook.

Old-Window Greenhouse

I know gardeners that have created beautiful greenhouses out of recycled windows. Look for remodeled houses that may throw away their old window frames and glasses. There may be pallets or scrap lumber from construction areas you can take for little to no money. Many construction sites want you to remove the junk they no longer need.

Umbrella Greenhouse

Reusing a clear umbrella to create a greenhouse for seedlings or small plants is a great project to begin your greenhouse journey. You need a clear umbrella, a PVC pipe, and a large pot. Attach the PVC pipe to the bottom of your pot. Make sure your pipe is wide enough to stick the long end of the umbrella into and tall sufficient to set the umbrella up over the pot. Fill your pot with soil and plants. Cut the handle off of the umbrella and place the spine into the pipe. Be sure you open the umbrella first. The umbrella should fit over the edges of the pot. It is best to use an umbrella with plastic prts, so they do not rust in the rain. Now you have created a quick and easy greenhouse.

Other Creative Repurposed Greenhouse Ideas

This is a novel idea, but if you have access to many PET plastic bottles, you can create a greenhouse by repurposing them. Simply tie them together to create walls of plastic bottles and fasten them to a frame to keep them steady.

You can also repurpose transparent plastic materials, such as clear plastic CD covers, food tray covers, and even discarded plastic sheets. You'll need to ensure that all your materials are safe to reuse and repurpose.

Greenhouse Location and Size

You're probably at the point where you can envision your greenhouse in your mind's eye. But there are more criteria to consider. Many gardeners immediately rush out to buy their materials without understanding how to choose the ideal location or determine the right size for their greenhouse.

Location

Ideally, the best site for your greenhouse is the area that receives the most sun, even during the colder months. Typically the southern side of your property gets the most sun, followed by the east side of the property. You can place your greenhouse in the southeast or southwest.

Another consideration is to find a location that protects your greenhouse from harsh elements like wind, rain, or snow. If you cannot protect your greenhouse from the elements, you must build a greenhouse strong enough to withstand them. Look for a flat area. Avoid any site at the base of a hill or slope.

Pay attention to anything that will block the sunlight from entering your greenhouse. Taller trees and artificial structures create shadows that can block sunlight. Don't forget: shadows are notably longer in winter than they are during summer.

You might also want to consider the plants you want to grow. For example, plants like blackberries, raspberries, and strawberries can still produce fruits in shady spots. If you plan to cultivate plants that need more sun, then you will need to adjust the location of your greenhouse.

Finally, think about the distance of your greenhouse from your main home. You may enjoy a long walk to the greenhouse on a beautiful summer day. But consider that walk in the rain or snow carrying a 10lb bag of soil. You want to make your greenhouse as convenient as possible.

Size

Greenhouses come in various sizes to fit your needs. The smallest greenhouse is about 4x6 feet and is perfect for starting seeds or bringing plants indoors for the winter. Larger greenhouses can be up to 24x48 feet and are great for growing vegetables or flowers.

The greenhouse you choose will depend on your space and what you plan to grow. A small greenhouse is a good option if you are starting out. To grow a lot of plants, you will need a larger greenhouse. My advice is to build the largest greenhouse you can afford. Greenhouse gardeners are ALWAYS looking for more space to grow.

8 Feet Wide

Hobby greenhouses usually start around eight feet wide from the outside. The interior width is shorter than eight feet, so you may need to factor this in. The typical setup for eight-foot-wide greenhouses is having two-foot-wide benches on each side. The center aisle is usually three feet wide. While this is an ideal size for a beginner, greenhouse gardeners quickly run out of space and dream up their next greenhouse.

10 Feet Wide

This is a popular option for many gardeners since the extra space allows more plants to be grown. This size is also perfect for most gardeners since it provides sufficient space for their plants while being maintained by an individual gardener.

12 to 20 Feet Wide

Greenhouses with this width range allow you to be creative with where and how you plant your garden. With this size greenhouse, you can add raised beds, seating areas, water features, or worktables.

Location and size are the final considerations when determining the greenhouse you will build. You are almost ready to build! Before you construct your greenhouse, there are a few more integral points to consider, particularly the internal systems required for effective operation.

Essential Systems for Every Greenhouse

A greenhouse needs four core systems to function optimally. These are heating and cooling, air, water, and light. Let's explore how each system factors into the overall effectiveness of your greenhouse.

Heating and Cooling

Heating and cooling are something every greenhouse gardener must manage. It is critical to maintaining optimal growing conditions. Greenhouses rely on the sun's heat to warm the air, but it can quickly become too hot for plants if not appropriately managed. A good heating and cooling system will regulate temperature and humidity levels to ensure your plants always have ideal growing conditions.

At the height of the summer, your focus is cooling. Gardeners may lift the panels on the roof or sides to let excess heat escape and increase airflow. If your greenhouse covering is PVC fabric, side panels can roll up to release heat. To decrease the sunlight entering the greenhouse, gardeners install shade cloth. For greenhouses in colder regions, it is essential to provide and lock in heat during these periods. Insulate and prevent heat from escaping.

If you plan to integrate a heating system into your greenhouse, here are ideas:

- You can use greenhouse heaters with a thermocouple sensor to maintain an even temperature throughout the year.

- Solar heaters are some of the best heating systems solutions since they are cost-effective, easy to install and use renewable energy without contributing to your carbon footprint.

- If you want a more affordable option consider placing barrel drums filled with dry gravel throughout your greenhouse. The gravel will absorb the heat during the day and release the warmth at night.

- Black or dark-colored pots will also retain heat. A great way to reuse old tires is to grow your plants inside.

Solar-powered systems are an excellent option for a greenhouse. They are versatile enough to adapt to a greenhouse's power requirements, and you never must fear your plants freezing because the power goes out.

There are two types of solar panels commercially available:

- **Polycrystalline Solar Cells-** These cells produce no silicon waste and are the more affordable option. However, they require a larger space to install.

- **Monocrystalline Solar Cells-** These cells need less installation space and are high-performing and more efficient but are also more expensive.

There are many considerations for a solar-powered heating system. The bigger your greenhouse, the more solar panels you will need to power its electrical needs. Also, consider the plants you want in the greenhouse because some plants require more heat than others. And finally, you must consider insulation. You want a greenhouse that will release heat in the summer and retain it in the winter.

Shades

Greenhouses can be subject to extreme temperatures when left exposed without shade. Shades help you control the heat and amount of light in your greenhouse. Too much heat or light can burn plants, so providing them with the right shade is essential. Here are considerations for you to think about.

Interior Shades

Interior greenhouse shades are ideal for modulating the sunlight entering your greenhouse. By regulating the intensity of incoming light, you can keep your environment cooler during summer and warmer in winter, making it much more comfortable to work year-round. With an array of interior shades to select from, it's easy to find the perfect match for your style and needs!

Shades come in different densities. When selecting an interior shade for your greenhouse, consider the plants you will be growing. Choose a less dense shade if growing plants need a lot of light.

Interior shades are installed in your greenhouse's interior and attached to the walls and ceilings. Interior shade kits usually come in various sizes to match the size of your greenhouse.

Benefits of Using Internal Shades

There are multiple advantages of placing shades in the interiors of your greenhouse. Factor them in when deciding if this option is the best for you.

- **Conserves energy.** The material of internal shades encourages radiant energy inside your greenhouse. Your greenhouse conserves heat during colder seasons, requiring less use of heating systems.

- **More durable.** The material lasts longer because your internal shades do not come into contact with wind, rain, or dirt.

- **Adjustable.** Most shades are individually sectioned, making them very convenient to close or open. This allows you to control the sunlight in your greenhouse.

Disadvantages of Using Internal Shades

- **Harder to install.** Some internal shades can be challenging to remove or install.

- **Does not block sunlight.** Harsh midday sun can damage your plants. Interior shades may not offer complete protection and can still allow the sunlight to harm your plants.

- **Does not reduce temperature.** The dark internal shades absorb radiant heat instead of reflecting it. Your greenhouse can end up hotter than expected.

- **Can reduce or block space.** Some interior shades can keep you from using hanging baskets or vertical planting systems.

External Shades

External greenhouse shades are an essential component in the summer. Shading outside the greenhouse helps keep the inside cooler and prevents the plants from getting scorched by the sun. A variety of different types of external shades can be used, including canvas, screens, and even trees!

Canvas shades are great if you want something easy to set up and take down. They can be attached to the outside greenhouse using ropes or bungee cords, then rolled up or taken down as needed.

When selecting your external shade, make sure that it is large enough to cover the entirety of the greenhouse and properly installed so it won't be swept away by gusts of wind.

Benefits of Using External Shades

- **Better cooling.** External shades offer better options for reducing internal greenhouse temperatures by blocking out the heat from the sun. Your greenhouse will remain cooler than the interior shades.

- **Blocks out harsh sun exposure.** External shades protect your greenhouse from overheating from excessive sun exposure heat.

- **Easy installation.** External shades are easier to set up because the fewer accessories and procedures are more straightforward.

Disadvantages of Using External Shades

- **Environmental exposure.** Your external shade is constantly exposed to heat, light, wind, rain, dirt, leaf deposits, and animal waste. These will eventually wear away your material despite its durability.

- **Reduced air circulation.** Ventilation can be an issue if your external shades prevent your greenhouse from having circulating air by covering raised panels or vents. However, leaving room between the shades and your greenhouse will solve this concern.

- **Not aesthetically pleasing.** Having external shades can make your greenhouse look dirty or untidy.

Pro Tips

- Increase your plants' warmth by using black or dark-colored pots because color attracts heat.

- Caulk your greenhouse to insulate and protect your plants from the weather, pests, and diseases.

Light

Every gardener knows that light is essential for plants to flourish. A greenhouse is built to allow that light into the structure. However, the natural light available can vary drastically with the seasons. If your locality experiences cooler seasons with longer nights, consider adding grow lamps to encourage the continued development of your plants. Grow lights are easily installed but will require an electrical source. Additional lighting and heat will give you more plant options for year-round gardening.

Water Access

Keeping your plants well-hydrated is the most essential element of successful gardening. Potted plants growing in greenhouses require more water than those planted in the ground. You should have ready access to water for your greenhouse. Before building a greenhouse, consider how you will access water to provide to your plants.

When selecting tap water for your plants, you must consider the precise location of your source and greenhouse. Additionally, plan ahead on how to successfully transport this water from its original site to your greenhouse.

The most eco-friendly watering system you can have for your plants is a rainwater collection system. This system collects rainwater directly from your downspouts and stores it in water barrels. Rainwater is more beneficial to your plants than tap water. In most localities in the U.S., fluoride is added to tap water. These and other additives to tap water make it less than ideal for your greenhouse plants.

If you go with a rainwater collection system, note:

- Before building your greenhouse, locate your downspouts so your rainwater collection system can be in or around your greenhouse.

- Remember to factor in the material and construction costs associated with the system.

- Ensure that your collected rainwater has a filter to keep out pests and debris.

Typically, the best rainwater tank for garden use should be able to store at least 40 gallons (151 liters) of rainwater. The tank should also be able to withstand cold and hot temperatures over a long-term period. Look for tanks made from polyethylene resin, which is UV-resistant, BPA-free, and does not mold, rot, or rust. Additionally, this material is solid and durable enough to weather harsh winters and even a strong force of impact without cracking. Material costs may vary depending on where you live.

Pro tip: Look for advertisements of people looking to get rid of their greenhouse to find low-cost heating, cooling, and electrical systems.

Airflow and Ventilation

Air circulation is another vital element of greenhouse design. Greenhouses can get very stuffy if the air isn't moving around correctly. Good air circulation will help prevent disease and pests and keep your plants healthy.

There are two ways you can encourage good ventilation in your greenhouse. Greenhouse gardeners often use a mix of natural and mechanical ventilation.

Natural Ventilation

This means using your greenhouse structure and design to encourage airflow. Gardeners manipulate structural components, such as windows and vents, to promote internal airflow. Natural ventilation may work in temperate climates, but mechanical ventilation is necessary if you live in a local area with more extreme winters and summers.

Mechanical Ventilation

Mechanical ventilation involves installing a fan ventilation system to help encourage airflow. It is often as simple as using fans in strategic places throughout the greenhouse for smaller greenhouses. Larger greenhouses may require a commercial ventilation system.

In either case, considering how air will move through your greenhouse before construction helps create an ideal environment for your plants.

Pro Tip

- Whichever method you choose, use screened ventilation to promote good airflow while keeping insects away from your plants.

Essential Tools for the Greenhouse

Successful gardeners know that the right tools are essential to providing plants the care they need to grow and thrive. Initially, I paid little attention to tools. But I soon learned there is no substitute for the right tool. I recommend these essential gardening tools to manage your greenhouse and your plants properly:

• A **thermometer and humidity gauge** are handy tools to check the internal temperature of your greenhouse. Digital thermometers are available that will send alerts to your phone if your greenhouse is too hot or too cold or if the humidity is too high or too low. These alerts help you intervene quickly before any damage can be done to your plants.

• One or more **gardening gloves** are needed to protect your hands from accidents and dirt. It is easy to disregard the need for gloves but wearing them will save you hours cleaning underneath your fingernails and protect your hands from cuts and other damage. Find a pair of gloves that are not too tight or too loose. Once you find a pair that works for you, buy multiples. Gardening gloves are easy to lose.

- The **hand trowel** is an essential gardening tool for potting, transplanting, and planting. You will use this tool non-stop initially as you organize and place your plants in pots or raised beds around your greenhouse.

- A pair of **pruning shears** helps you shape and trim your plants to promote growth. Initially, I used scissors. Trust me! They do not work and are a good pair of pruning shears. Maintain your pruning shears using a scouring pad to clean and remove rust.

- A **gardening fork** helps you penetrate the ground to aerate the soil.

- A **shovel** can be your best friend for digging and loosening garden materials.

- A **rake** is a perfect tool for removing unwanted materials while leveling the surface of your soil.

- A **wheelbarrow** might be an incredible essential tool. However, imagine how you will transport large loads of garden materials like bags of soil or large plants. You will save yourself time and energy transporting materials from the car to your greenhouse if you use a wheelbarrow. It is truly an essential tool.

Plan how you will store your tools. The organization of your greenhouse is critical. When planning your greenhouse, you must identify work and storage space. Make a habit of putting all your tools back in one place when done gardening. I've lost too many gardening tools to count and several pairs of gardening gloves. The inconvenience of not having the tools I needed and the cost of replacing tools soon added up. I became much more successful as a gardener when I organized my tools.

You will also need to clean and maintain your tools. Use a scouring pad to rub away any rust. A simple solution of one parts bleach to nine parts water in a large bucket will disinfect tools. It took a lot to remember to clean and disinfect my tools. I've learned to do it with the change of seasons. I think about starting fresh when planting my spring and summer garden or my fall and winter garden. Remember, greenhouse gardening is year-round!

How Much Does It Cost?

I've been fascinated by greenhouses since I was a little kid. I remember seeing the glass building with all the pretty plants and thinking it was the coolest thing ever. So, when I started my garden, I knew I needed a greenhouse. But I quickly learned that greenhouses are not cheap! They can be darn expensive.

The cost of materials for a basic greenhouse can range from $400 to $1,200. But if you want a fancier greenhouse made of wood or metal, you're looking at a much higher price tag—anywhere from $2,500 to $5,000. And that's not even considering the cost of labor! If you hire someone to build your greenhouse for you, you can expect to pay an additional $1,000 to $2,500.

There are ways to save money when building a greenhouse. If you're handy and have some basic carpentry skills, you can save on labor costs by doing it yourself. And if you're willing to get creative with your materials, there are plenty of ways to use recycled and repurposed items for your greenhouse—like using old windows or recycled PVC pipe for the frame.

You can purchase an inexpensive plastic greenhouse from stores like Target and Walmart for less than $100. You may want a small one to understand how to manage it. The materials are not eco-friendly. But it's a place to start. Once you are more confident and expand, you can determine how much you want to invest.

My first greenhouse was an Ikea Greenhouse. Yes, I scoured the internet for a template. I bought a used Ikea glass cabinet from Facebook, grow lights, and fans from Amazon. I even insulated the doors. I spent about $200. It was a lot of fun building my greenhouse. My family and friends are still amazed at what I have done. I still have it today. Building a greenhouse is not cheap—there's no way around that. But it is worth the investment if you're passionate about gardening and want to extend your growing season or grow plants that wouldn't thrive outdoors in your climate.

The Takeaway

Building a greenhouse takes lots of planning and organization, especially if you care about its impact on the earth. There are many decisions to make, from the greenhouse frame to its covering and even into how you will provide water, ventilation, heat, and cooling. There are a few ideas to remember to keep your greenhouse environmentally sound. Use the most eco-friendly materials to build a sturdy, long-lasting greenhouse. Use solar panels to power your greenhouse. A rainwater collection system is excellent but has a backup. Heating and cooling your greenhouse during the first year will be a learning process. Proper ventilation will help with cooling the summers and is vital to the health of your plants in the winter. A greenhouse can cost $400 - $2000 or more to build. It is expensive but worth the investment. To cut back on costs, look for recycled building materials such as used windows. Building it yourself can also save you money on labor costs. And finally, don't forget to purchase the essential tools of the trade if you don't already have them. Building a greenhouse can easily be overwhelming. If you take your time and create a good ,plan you will move through the process with ease.

Take Action

1. Determine your budget as well as the structural style and materials best suited to your greenhouse needs.

2. Identify other necessary systems and tools for your greenhouse, such as heating and cooling, lighting, water supply, or ventilation.

3. Consider the location and size of your greenhouse, considering factors like weather conditions and space. This is a case when bigger is better.

4. Research DIY greenhouse building techniques, such as utilizing unconventional materials or repurposing existing structures for greenhouses to cut costs and reduce the impact on the environment.

5. Once your greenhouse is built, maintain it regularly to ensure optimal growing conditions and long-term sustainability.

Chapter 2

How to Use Every Inch of Your Greenhouse for Plants

Before considering setting up a greenhouse, please think about a few things before starting. In this chapter, we'll discuss how to maximize space in your greenhouse for productivity. We'll also talk about the pros and cons of different greenhouse layouts and how to choose the right one for your needs. After reading this chapter, you'll be well-versed in the various greenhouse construction methods and how to maximize your space utilization.

Let's get started!

Greenhouse Staging

Maximize your greenhouse's potential with staging! With proper organization, you can grow an abundance of plants in a confined space. Staging is the term that gardeners use to describe the structures inside the greenhouse. These structures can be tables, benches, and shelves. You can choose from permanent, moveable, or a combination of both staging styles. Staging provides more space to work with, an area to keep things tidy, and can be made from different materials. Well-planned greenhouse staging will save you a lot of time and effort later, especially as the number of plants increases.

To help you choose the right staging option to suit your needs, let's look at the advantages and disadvantages of each type.

Greenhouse Benches

Greenhouse benches are an essential part of any greenhouse. They provide a place to put plants to receive the maximum light possible. Benches also help to keep the plants warm by trapping heat from the sun. They come in many types and are made of different materials.

Slatted Bench

Slatted benches in a greenhouse offer many benefits. They improve air circulation around the plants, which can help to prevent fungal diseases. They also make it easier to control the temperature within the greenhouse and provide extra drainage for water-loving plants. Finally, slatted benches can make it easier to access your plants, especially if you have a lot.

However, slatted benches in a greenhouse can create shady areas perfect for moss and algae to grow. If not cleaned regularly, these areas can become slip hazards. In addition, slatted benches can make it difficult to water plants evenly and may cause irrigation problems.

Netted Bench

The netted bench in a greenhouse offers several benefits. They keep the soil from mixing, help to control pests, and improve air circulation. The netting also helps to support the plant as it grows. These factors contribute to a healthier planet and a more successful harvest.

This bench has a metal wire netting on top to allow airflow. Many bench models also come in plastic, making them more durable than metal wire netting. However, most gardeners prefer metal wire netting material since it is easier to disinfect over plastic.

Netted benches are unsuitable for automatic watering systems. Much like the slatted bench, this model will be challenging when used as a workstation.

Also, be careful when placing your pots on netted benches. The weight of your potted plants can cause the wire netting to sag. Wire metal netting can rust and corrode as time goes by. To prevent this, coat your wire metal netting with rust-proof paint.

You will also need to be careful when using metal wire netting since it can have sharp edges. Ensure that all ends and edges are tied up and smooth to prevent rips on skin and clothes.

Solid Bench

The solid bench is mainly used as a workstation. It usually comes in a corrugated or flat form. It is the strongest of all benches, so it is appropriate for placing heavier materials. They can even be used for irrigation. Some solid benches have a shallow lip you can fill with water for an automatic watering system.

Ranging from wood and metal to plastic materials, the solid bench is constructed with a vast array of diverse materials. Plastic materials are lightweight, durable, and portable. Unlike metal, rust does not present a problem for solid plastic benches. Additionally, solid benches conserve heat during the colder winter seasons.

Despite their ease of use and low maintenance, solid plastic benches are harder to disinfect And are not fireproof, making your greenhouse challenging to insure.

Generally, keeping potted plants on solid benches for a prolonged period is discouraged. Solid benches make air circulation and drainage tricky, which could harm your plants.

Material Types

There is no magic answer to materials. Each comes with pros and cons. To choose the best materials for your staging, determine the plants you will grow and the activities you will do in the greenhouse.

Benches come in various materials, which can influence your budget and layout. You will need to consider their durability, weight capacity, height, airflow, drainage, and cost, among other factors.

Below are some of the most popular materials you can employ for staging:

Wood

Choose wood highly resistant to rot and decay. The most popular wood choices for benches are cedar, cypress, locust, redwood, and teak. Treated lumber is also an excellent choice for wood benches. It will not decay for around 10 to 15 years. To further prevent decay, you can coat your wooden benches with preservatives, such as copper naphthenate, which is safe around plants and animals.

Your wooden bench can be pure wood or a combination of metal and other materials. However, when wooden materials are combined with metal parts, the metal parts can corrode faster than usual. Most wooden benches have welded or expanded metal wire. The expanded metal wire is more expensive but does not sag, unlike welded wire.

Additionally, wood can easily warp due to environmental factors, such as water, heat, and light. Wood absorbs moisture quickly, requiring higher regular maintenance. Wood can also host insects and diseases from fungi and other pathogens.

Metal

Some benches come in pure metal materials, while others have wood or plastic components. Galvanized metal lasts longer than wood, making it more durable and resistant to decay and rot. However, metal benches cost more. Metal benches require less maintenance than wooden ones.

Aluminum is an excellent material for your staging because it is durable and lightweight and provides good airflow and drainage. It is resistant to rust, making maintenance almost unnecessary. Unfortunately, aluminum benches cannot support large or heavy pots.

Most aluminum benches come with galvanized steel, making the structure the best of both worlds. Galvanized steel gives benches strength. The cost can be expensive, although it is a good investment.

Pro Tip

- To make the best of this staging, paint your aluminum benches white to reflect more light.

Plastic

Plastic benches are quickly becoming more available in gardening and big box stores. The material is lightweight and durable. These qualities make prefabricated plastic benches ideal for portable staging. Some models even come with rollers. Maintaining plastic benches is more manageable than wood ones.

Nevertheless, it is essential to be prudent when choosing plastic benches for your staging. Plastic bars are not as durable or as strong as wood and metal. Plastic benches are not environmentally friendly, so you should have an excellent reason to purchase them.

Concrete

Poured concrete benches are permanent greenhouse fixtures that are durable and highly resistant to corrosion, rot, and decay. You can increase its durability by reinforcing your concrete benches with steel or metal rods. Concrete is a wonderful material for staging but can be expensive. However, you will need to plan the design well because it will be a permanent fixture. Also, think about drainage holes to prevent stagnant water.

Pallets and Cement Block Supports

This is an affordable option you can explore. The mix of inexpensive wooden pallets and cement blocks gives this bench the right strength, durability, support, air circulation, and portability without costing too much. If you prefer this option, ensure that your pallets are treated to prevent decay and rot.

Some gardeners use different materials to support their benches, such as steel poles, plastic supports, and wooden legs. Each material will always have its advantages and disadvantages. Know what you need and choose your materials.

Pro Tips

- Whichever material you work with, remember to keep the benches to a maximum height and width of three feet (91.44 cm) when placed against a wall.

- For freestanding benches, you can allocate a maximum width of six feet (182.88 cm). This will allow you to accommodate the majority of your planting activities comfortably.

- Make sure that your bench can support at least 25 pounds per square foot area (11.34 kilograms per square meter).

- Look for a two-tier staging with a removable bottom to keep your tools and trays for more storage.

The Benefits of Raised Bed Gardening

Raised beds are enclosed soil structures raised above the ground. The enclosure can be made of wood, concrete, rock, plastic, and other materials.

The size and shape of raised beds largely depend on the gardener, making these enclosures versatile. Raised beds are great garden options, with many advantages to a greenhouse.

Flexibility

Raised beds allow you to create patterns and layouts in your greenhouse that can be challenging with other structures. They can be easily assembled and disassembled to allow you to change their location as your needs change.

Better Soil Conditions

The design of raised beds will enable you to control the soil conditions. Soil management is vital to creating the best growing conditions for your plants. Raised beds allow you to make the ideal soil for your plants to grow in terms of drainage, texture, and pH level. Additionally, raised beds have fresher and healthier soil for your plants while reducing insects and weeds.

Optimal Growing Conditions

Raised beds are ideal for growing vegetables as the entire plan will receive equal sunlight. When grown on shelves, the light received by the plant is uneven. The temperature of the soil in raised beds stays warmer than the soil on the ground. This is especially advantageous for unheated greenhouses because it allows the gardener to extend the growing season.

Less Work

Raised beds encourage you to be more productive by eliminating the strenuous physical work usually associated with gardening. No more fussing over weeding, tilling, or stooping to attend to your in-ground garden beds - those days are a thing of the past! With raised beds, you must put in less effort to maintain your garden.

Pro Tips

- In raised beds, don't place plants too near each other to avoid their roots overcrowding and competing for nutrients.

Container Growing

There are many benefits to container gardening in a greenhouse. One benefit is that you can grow a wider variety of plants. Another advantage is that you can control the environment, leading to a higher yield. Furthermore, container gardening in a greenhouse can provide additional protection against pests and diseases that may otherwise harm your plants. Finally, it can extend the growing season and allow you to grow plants year-round. These benefits make container gardening in a greenhouse ideal for many gardeners.

Optimized Garden Space

Gardening in containers makes it simpler to shift plants to make more room in your greenhouse. Plants cultivated in containers are typically more portable, allowing you to move them to locations ideal for their development.

Going Vertical

Vertical gardening, as the name implies, entails growing plants in vertical rows rather than horizontally. Plants are stacked one on top of another, whether it's via shelving or vertical planters. There are several advantages to vertical gardening in a greenhouse. One advantage is that it takes up less room, which is helpful if you have a small greenhouse or only have limited growing space. Another advantage is that it can improve air circulation around your plants.

It's now easier than ever to explore the limitless possibilities of vertical gardening! With a multitude of options available, you can enjoy growing fruits and vegetables in more creative ways. Further, recent technology and farming methods have made gardening even more efficient without requiring too many resources.

Greenhouse Shelving System

This involves stacking your greenhouse plants on shelves. This works best if your shelves are tiered to allow sunlight exposure for plants at the lower levels. Place this system on the side of your greenhouse that receives the most sun during the day.

Vertical Pallet System

A great way to reuse a pallet is to use it for vertical gardening. Start by covering the back of the pallet with wood or landscape fabric. Then lay it flat on its back and fill it with soil or compost—plant leafy green in the space between the boards. Stand the pallet on its side. You now have an inexpensive vertical planter. This is a great space to grow herbs and leafy greens.

Pallets are affordable solutions that allow you to have a vertical garden. However, remember that the material can eventually rot and decay. You'll need to be vigilant, as rotting wood invites pests and disease. This method provides a rustic look to your greenhouse and may be the perfect approach when your budget is limited.

Vertical Planter System

These come in all shapes and sizes and are readily available in retail garden stores. Think of a strawberry pot, and you will understand the design. The structure utilizes a centralized soil model that allows plants to grow from the sides. Gardeners are creative. They have used large PVC pipes filled with compost and soil. Then cut a few alternating holes from top to bottom, and viola, vertical gardening. Watering is even easier because you will just water from the top and allow gravity to pull the water down toward the plants. Make sure the structure is well-supported because it can get top-heavy.

Fabric Pockets

Vertical gardens grown in fabric pockets are easy to install and maintain. They are typically made of lightweight material recycled to resemble felt. The fibrous material allows water to circulate and drain while enabling the air inside to aerate the roots of the plants.

You can buy them from commercial garden centers and suppliers. You can create your own using landscape fabric and burlap sacks.

Hanging Baskets

Even hanging baskets can be helpful and efficient containers for gardeners with limited space. Hang some baskets overhead and allow trailing or vining plants to tumble down from their containers.

This method is affordable, easy to install, and highly portable. Ensure that your baskets are durable and can carry the weight of your plants.

Hydroponic Systems

Hydroponics gardening means using soil-less systems to grow plants. It sounds very futuristic, but it has been around since 1937. The system is efficient because everything is under controlled conditions. Plants and vegetables grow to be healthy without toxic chemical exposure or pesticides. With the vertical hydroponics system, the roots of the plants are placed in removable cups submerged in a circulating water-based nutrient solution.

Some gardeners even incorporate aquaponics into a hydroponic system. Aquaponics is where fish are introduced into the hydroponic system, allowing the waste of the fish to act as additional nutrient sources for the plants. A hydroponics system can be costly. This is an excellent investment because it pays off eventually. In addition, weigh the operational costs this system demands, such as water, electricity, and general supplies. This method will require less maintenance time, and your output will improve.

Ideal Plants for Vertical Gardening

Vertical gardening plants are diverse. The list of plants ideal for vertical gardening is much more extensive than you imagine. You'll be surprised at the different types of vegetation that make excellent candidates for vertical growing. Here are some of our favorites, in no particular order, to try your hand at growing vertically.

Vegetables

Beans, baby carrots, miniature cucumbers, miniature eggplants, garlic, miniature onions, peas, compact-variety peppers, baby potatoes, baby pumpkins, shallots, baby squash, cascading or patio tomatoes, cabbage, kale, lettuce, mustard greens, spinach, Swiss chard

Fruits

Baby cantaloupe, mini kiwi, passionfruit, baby watermelon, midget muskmelon, and strawberries

Herbs

Basil, bergamot, borage, chervil, chives, cilantro, cumin, dill, lemon balm, lemon grass, marjoram, mint, nasturtium, oregano, parsley, rosemary, sage, savory, stevia, thyme, and wheatgrass

Medicinal and Aromatherapeutic

Aloe vera, borage, calendula, catmint, chamomile, echinacea, scented geranium, goldenseal, hyssop, lavender, nasturtium, patchouli, sweet woodruff, yarrow

The Takeaway

The information above shows many ways to optimize space in a greenhouse. Using benches, raised beds, containers, and vertical planting, you can fit more plants into a smaller space. Hydroponics allows you to grow plants in less space, making it an excellent option for greenhouses.

Take Action

1. Determine the staging that will work best for your space and your budget.

2. Is your greenhouse best suited to raised beds or container gardening? Can you mix both?

3. Are shelves and benches best suited to your greenhouse?

4. Will vertical staging maximize your greenhouse space? If so, how will you organize it?

5. Do you want to explore hydroponics?

CHAPTER 3

FROM SEED TO TABLE: HOW TO GROW AND ENJOY FRESH FRUITS AND VEGETABLES

Growing your first vegetables in a greenhouse is an exciting and rewarding experience. Something is satisfying about nurturing little seedlings into full-grown, healthy plants that bear delicious fruits and vegetables.

As you care for your plants, you will develop a sense of pride and accomplishment as they grow bigger and stronger each day. And when it comes time to harvest your bounty, there is nothing more satisfying than enjoying the fruits (literally!) of your labor.

Many greenhouse gardeners want to grow their fruits and vegetables from seeds. This chapter provides all the advice you need to get those seedlings off to a great start. From germination techniques and direct sow methods to tips for caring for growing plants and knowing when to harvest your fruits and veggies, this chapter has everything you need to cultivate a flourishing greenhouse garden successfully.

The Best Fruits and Vegetables to Plant in your Greenhouse

A greenhouse is about creating the best environment for your fruits and vegetables to thrive. But determining what to grow in your greenhouse can be overwhelming. Some of the most popular produce grown in greenhouses include tomatoes, cucumbers, peppers, leafy greens, melons, and juicy strawberries - providing a delicious source of freshness for any meal! These vegetables thrive in the warm, humid conditions found in greenhouses. These plants are ideal because they ripen quickly and can be harvested sooner than when not grown in a greenhouse.

One might wonder if you can grow fruit trees in a greenhouse. The answer is YES! To grow fruit trees in your greenhouse, you must mimic their native environment. In northern climates, this means HEAT. So include a heating system in your greenhouse if you plan to grow fruit trees.

Though some fruit trees cannot be grown in a greenhouse, the list of fruit trees that can is long. It includes citrus, figs, pomegranates, mangos, papayas, bananas, avocados, olives, and almonds. Remember, growing fruit trees is a long-term project, especially if you grow them from seed. Harvest times are measured in terms of years, not months.

Planting Seeds

There's something special about planting seeds. It's a magical moment when you take that tiny little seed, add some water and dirt, and watch it grow into a full-fledged plant. And if you're lucky, that plant will produce delicious fruits or vegetables you can enjoy.

Planting seeds is not only rewarding, but it's also a great way to save money. Why buy expensive plants at the nursery when you can grow them from seed? Plus, you'll have a greater variety of plants if you start from seed.

Germination

Germination is when a new organism grows from a seed. The seed needs soil, water, oxygen, and warmth to germinate. There are two ways to get your seeds into the ground: directly sow them or start a nursery with seedling trays and transplant the sprouts when they're ready.

Seedling Trays

Seedling trays are an easy and efficient way to germinate seeds. Using a seedling tray, you can control the environment by adding the perfect heat and humidity, which is essential for getting your seeds to germinate successfully. They are easy to move around the greenhouse, allowing you to find the right spot for them. Additionally, a seed tray helps you organize your seeds and track which ones you've planted.

Some benefits of using seed trays include

- They help to protect the seeds from pests and diseases.
- They provide a warm and humid environment ideal for germination.
- They allow you to control the water and fertilizer that the seeds receive.
- They make it easy to transplant the seedlings into pots or other containers when they are ready to be moved.
- Since they can be reused, these options are cost-effective.

Reusing or recycling everyday items such as seed-starting trays is not only cost-effective, but it's also eco-friendly.

· You can use various objects as makeshift seedling trays around your house.

- It turns out those old egg cartons have a use after all! Remember to give them a good wash before using them.
- Yogurt containers and take-out coffee cups are also

great for starting seeds. Poke a few holes in the bottom for drainage.

- Keep things clean and sterile by using recycled cans or plastic bottles. Rinse them out and remove the labels.

Other household items that can be used as seed trays include toilet paper rolls, aluminum trays, cardboard boxes, and even empty eggshells. If you buy seedling trays, please remember to take care of them so you can use them repeatedly.

Direct Sowing Your Seeds

Direct sowing, or direct seeding, is planting seeds right in the garden instead of starting them indoors or growing them in a seed tray to transplant later.

For the most successful planting of your seeds, plant them directly into the ground 6-8 weeks before the final frost date in your locale. Doing so will yield beautiful blossoms and bountiful harvests!

Determining the first and last frost for your location is easy. If you live in the US, use the USDA plant hardiness zone map and enter your postal code to find your correct zone. The map has ten zones showing each area's average climatic conditions.

The zones will help you understand how well your plant will tolerate cold conditions. The zones also help you determine the ideal times to plant your seeds. Seed packets also normally display this information, so your selection should be easy to make.

Some cool-season crops are ideal for direct sowing, especially root vegetables and crops that prefer to start in warm soil. If you plan to grow warm-season crops, the perfect time to sow them directly is after the frost date and when the soil has warmed up.

While some crops are not particular about being sown indoors or outdoors, some will thrive better when planted directly in the ground. Transplant shock can cause vegetables and herbs to grow poorly or even perish due to root system disturbance.

Preparing Your Garden for Direct Sowing

Remove all weeds from your soil and check if the soil is compacted. If it is, dig it up to keep it workable and loose. At the beginning of the chapter, you can improve your soil with compost and other soil amendments. This is best done during the fall. This way, your soil will be ready by spring.

Sowing Your Seeds

For this step, we suggest preparing the following:

- Seeds
- Tags
- Tray

- Notebook

- Marking pen

- Trowel

When ready, you'll need to grab your direct seed-sowing materials and go to your gardening area. Your tray will help you keep your activity organized by giving you ample access to seeds, tags, markers, and notes to keep track of what you're planting.

Depending on the seed type and size, you can scatter or bury each into the soil. We sprinkle tiny seeds, while larger ones get buried in the soil individually. Once the seeds are in the ground, cover them with a thin layer of soil.

You can purchase the seeding square to make your direct sowing easier. It is a template laid over the garden soil with spaced holes to indicate where the seeds should be sown.

I suggest placing a tag or several once you've planted a row to remember what you planted and where you planted them. You can even write special instructions as a reminder of the proper care for each plant.

Some crops perfect for direct sowing include:

Crops	Annual Flowers
Beans, including lima bush and pole	Bachelor's buttons
Beet	Cosmos
Carrot	Marigolds
Corn	Nasturtiums
Lettuce	Poppies
Melon	Zinnias
Peas	
Radish	Herbs
Squash, including spaghetti squash pumpkins	Basil can be started indoors.
Turnip	Cilantro
Zucchini	Dill

Fruit trees have unique needs. They do better when grown in containers. Containers allow you to move your trees inside and outside the greenhouse, depending on the weather. The best fruit trees for containers are apple, apricot, cherry, pear, and plum. Ensure their containers are the correct sizes to allow optimal root and tree growth.

However, if you use seedling trays, the soil you should use for germination depends on the plant. Some plants prefer sandy soil, while others prefer clay. The best way to determine what kind of soil to purchase is by researching on the internet or asking someone at your local nursery.

Testing Seeds for Germination

Fresh seeds rarely need to be tested for germination as they have higher chances of sprouting. However, if your seeds are over six months old, you may need to check for their viability.

Place your seeds on one side of a moist paper towel. Fold the damp paper towel to cover the seeds, place the paper towel inside a plastic bag, and seal the plastic bag.

Keep the sealed plastic bag in a warm area. Mist the paper towel occasionally to keep it from drying out. By the end of seven days, viable seeds will have germinated.

Starting Fruit Seeds

Fruit seeds are different and require more patience. Germination takes longer, and many fruit seeds need a cold period known as stratification. The best way to germinate fruit seeds is to plant them in a pot filled with a moist, sterile seed starting mix. Position the pot in a warm area and ensure the soil remains moist. Once the seedlings sprout, move them to a sunny spot. Do extensive research on the internet and talk to other gardeners to learn how to start your seeds. Because starting fruit seeds is difficult, buy a seedling from the store.

Thinning Out Seedlings

Once your seeds sprout, you may notice seeds clumping and growing together. Removing seedlings that grow in a group is best to keep them from competing for water and nutrition. This process is called thinning. Thinning out your seedlings will ensure that your seedlings grow healthier and sturdier. Whether grown on the ground or in seedling trays, keep one seedling in each slot.

To thin out your seedlings, prepare small pruning shears or gardening scissors. Sterilize with rubbing alcohol before you start. With the sterilized tool, snip off the seedlings at the base of their stems. Leave the roots alone to avoid damaging the root of nearby plants. It is preferable to take out the smallest seedlings. However, if you're unsure, you can randomly take them out. The earlier you thin out your seedlings, the better their chances for healthy growth.

Transplanting Seedlings from the Tray

Knowing when to transplant your seedlings is as important as knowing how to transplant them. Here are valuable guidelines you should remember to ensure your seedlings are ready to be transplanted.

Pick the Perfect Time

Your seedlings' first two leaves are called cotyledons or seed leaves. These initial sets of leaves are in simple and smooth oval shapes--sometimes barely visible on the plant.

The seedlings' true leaves will be the next set of leaves to sprout. They'll look like tiny versions of regular-sized plant leaves. Subsequent sets of true leaves will appear too. When you see this, it's time to transplant your seedlings.

Transplanting to a Larger Container

When choosing a container for your seedling, ensure it is big enough for the roots to expand. The container should also have drainage holes to allow excess water to escape. As for soil, it is best to use a potting mix specifically designed for plants. These mixes are usually lighter and fluffier than garden soil, making them easier for roots to grow.

Transplanting Outside

Many gardeners use their Greenhouse to start seedlings and transplant them to an outside garden. If this is your intent, you'll need to know when you'll need o plant your garden outdoors. Planting will depend on your climate or your plant's hardiness zone. Residents of areas with an extended growing season can start planting as early as March or April, allowing them to enjoy the fruits (and vegetables) of their labor sooner. However, if you live in a location with a shorter growing season, you will need to wait until May or June to plant your garden.

Harden Off Your Seedlings

Before you transplant, harden off your seedlings. This refers to allowing seedlings to adapt to their new environment. By giving them time to adjust, you ensure that your seedlings do not experience transplant shock and can quickly acclimate to their new homes.

The process takes seven to ten days, during which your plants are slowly introduced to their new surroundings. Begin by placing your seedlings in a shady area for two to three hours. Make sure that they are not exposed to strong winds. Bring the seedlings back in after a couple of hours.

On the second day, take out your seedlings for three to four hours in a less shady area than the first. Do the same for a week or more to get your seedlings acclimated to their future homes.

In the last few days, leave your seedlings out overnight, so they get used to the cooler night temperatures.

Transplanting Your Seedlings

Now, your seedlings are ready for their new homes. The ideal condition to transplant your seedlings outside will be mild weather with some clouds. Ideally, transplant early in the morning. If this is difficult, you can transplant your seedlings late in the afternoon. The key is to avoid the harsh afternoon sun when the weather is too cold or hot. The shock might harm or kill your seedlings.

Transplant your seedling into a hole neither too deep nor too shallow. You'll know the perfect depth when the seedling sits slightly above ground level.

Turn over your seedling tray and gently tap on the bottom to loosen the soil. Keep the seedlings' soil and roots intact. Gently remove the seedling from the tray without damaging the leaves or the stems.

You may notice that some roots are tightly coiled. Before you place your seedlings in the new soil, loosen the coiled roots gently to help them spread.

Ensure the new soil is loose to promote aeration and root growth. You can slowly place your seedling in the hole and pat it to secure it.

After Transplant

Once your seedlings are in their new homes, water the soil. If your soil is well-draining, it should feel moist or damp. Avoid getting your newly transplanted seedlings sitting in water-soaked soil to reduce the risk of root rot.

You can add some fertilizer if you'd like but dilute the dose to avoid shocking the seedlings.

Watering Your Seedlings

Keeping your plants hydrated is important, especially when they're still seedlings. As a general rule, always keep the soil of your seedlings moist or damp, but never wet.

To do this, stick your finger into the soil about an inch. If the ground feels moist, you don't need water yet. If the soil is dry, then it's time to give your seedlings a drink.

If you prefer a more precise method of determining the moisture level of your soil, you can always use a moisture meter. These commercially available meters can be quickly buried in the soil near your plant. The moisture meter will soon let you know whether the soil needs watering by looking at the gauge.

Most gardeners mistakenly include the leaves when watering their plants. Unless the water dries incredibly quickly in your area, this can lead to your plants developing burns or fungal infections.

A drip irrigation system is a wonderful option for dry arid environments. It is also a great watering system for plants with shallow roots since the release is slow and done over time. Plants with shallow roots, such as strawberries, peppers, and tomatoes, benefit from the slow water release rate.

Taking Care of Growing Plants

Overwatering and Underwatering

One of the consistent activities you will do to take care of your growing plants is water. Different plants need different amounts of water.

First, research how much water your plants need. Overwatering will result in the leaves getting limp and yellow. This is usually caused by standing water or soil with too much clay. You can remedy these by ensuring your soil is loose and well-draining and having a plant container with excellent drainage.

Underwatering causes the leaves to wilt and dry. If the leaves are still green, water your plant immediately. However, if it looks like the plant is dead, gently check the roots for life. You may bring your plant back to life if the roots are still alive.

Pruning Your Plants

Many plants need pruning to encourage bushier growth and healthier produce. Pruning improves the ventilation around the plants while allowing more light to reach the other parts of the plants. Pruning also keeps your plants from becoming too large and overtaking your greenhouse. There are five ways to prune your plants:

Thinning. We've already covered this when we touched on growing seedlings. However, you can also thin mature plants to promote better air circulation and reduce fungal infections. Many plants benefit from thinning since it encourages them to produce more flowers and fruits. A prime candidate for thinning is squash. Their densely packed vines can breed fungus and disease.

Heading. This refers to removing the flower buds of your plants to encourage healthier growth. Plants ideal for heading include peppers, eggplants, and other plants that produce flowers before fruits. You can also head off your non-flowering plants by clipping off a stem or branch to encourage fuller and bushier growth.

Pinching. To make your plants more robust and increase production, pinch off the growing tips. This will result in a smaller plant but better yields for chili peppers, green beans, tomatoes, and other vegetables.

Clipping. Clipping is when you cut off the tips of a plant. Clip a plant to concentrate growth in the center of the plant.

This prevents plants from growing in unorthodox angles and helps preserve their overall health. Vegetables like kale and tomatoes are kept bushier and more compact through clipping, allowing more air and sunlight to pass through them. If you're consistent with your clipping, you can avoid getting support structures (trellises) for many plants that would otherwise need them.

Shearing. Some plants, like raspberries, grow denser when sheared during late winter or early spring. Leaves, flowers, and fruits will come back quicker once spring arrives.

Pro Tip

- When pruning, please remember to use sterilized tools. Sterilization will prevent pests, bacteria, and fungi from contaminating your plants.

Pruning Fruit Trees

One of the most common questions about pruning fruit trees is, "when should I prune my trees?" The answer to that question is contingent on the fruit tree you have. Late winter or early spring is the optimal period for pruning deciduous fruit trees that shed leaves in autumn. Prune before the tree buds to ensure healthy growth. This lets you see the tree's structure and make pruning cuts. You risk damaging new growth if you wait until the tree has budded.

To ensure optimal health and fruit production, evergreen trees must be pruned regularly. The best time to get this done is shortly after the tree has bloomed, in late spring or early summer. This ensures that you don't remove any potential buds or flowers that could turn into fruit later in the season.

There are two main cuts for pruning fruit trees: thinning cuts and heading cuts. Thinning cuts are made by removing entire branches back to the tree's main trunk or scaffold branches (large, horizontal branches). Heading cuts are made by cutting off the tips of branches. Both types of cuts serve different purposes and should be used.

Thinning cuts open the tree's interior, allowing for more sunlight, air circulation, and overall health. The goal is to remove branches that are overcrowding other branches or growing at odd angles. Heading cuts should be used only sparingly and as a last resort. Heading cuts are used to direct the growth of a branch but should never be used on larger branches or scaffold branches.

When to Harvest Your Fruits and Vegetables

There is no greater pleasure than eating the fruits and vegetables you grew from scratch. Knowing the right time to harvest can be the most valuable information you can get. Here are the harvesting guidelines to use with your garden.

- **Size.** Mature fruits and vegetables are larger than their unripe versions.

- **Color.** Each fruit and vegetable will have its indication of ripeness in terms of color. Usually, the colors of ripe fruits and vegetables will be full, deep, and vibrant.

- **Fragrance.** Most fruits, like peaches and apples, emit scents that indicate their ripeness. Vegetables do not give out any fragrance.

- **Softness.** The majority of fruits will be firm but give slightly when pressed. However, vegetables are hard, even when ripe.

- **Taste.** Ripe fruits taste sweet, whereas unripe ones taste tasteless or sour. Vegetables produce their flavors when cooked.

Here is a list of when the most commonly found fruits and vegetables that are grown in a greenhouse should be harvested:

Lettuce- You can harvest lettuce leaves as soon as they are big enough to eat. For a continuous supply, sow seeds every few weeks.

Tomatoes- Tomatoes are usually ready to harvest about four months after planting. Check the color of the fruit – it should be a deep red.

Cucumbers-Cucumbers are usually ready to harvest about two months after planting. Look for fruits that are dark green and have reached the desired size.

Peppers- Peppers are usually ready to harvest about three months after planting. Look for fruits that are bright in color and have reached the desired size.

Eggplants- Eggplants are usually ready to harvest about four months after planting. Look for fruits that are shiny and have reached the desired size.

Squash- Squash is usually ready to harvest about three months after planting. Look for fruits that are dull in color and have reached the desired size.

Pumpkins- Pumpkins are usually ready to harvest about four months after planting. Look for fruits that are dull in color and have reached the desired size.

Strawberries- Depending on the variety, strawberries should take about 4-6 weeks after flowering. Berries should be a deep red and cut at the stem to avoid damage.

Raspberries- Raspberries take about ten weeks to produce fruit. You can tell raspberries are ripe when they are soft and dark. Raspberries will get no riper after they are picked, so don't pick them before they are ripe.

Dwarf Fruit Trees- Dwarf fruit trees take two to three years to mature to produce fruit. After the tree matures, you can expect fruit once a year.

Avocado Trees- Growing your own avocado tree can take significant time and patience. Depending on if you begin with a seed, it may be as long as 13 years before the tree is mature enough to bear fruit. Generally, an avocado plant takes three to four years until maturity.

Olive Trees- Olive trees take three years to bear fruit. Then only bear significant fruit every other year.

The Takeaway

Growing your first fruits and vegetables in a greenhouse is an exhilarating experience that gives you a sense of pride and satisfaction as your plants flourish under your care. Understanding the best techniques for planting seeds, caring for seedlings, and harvesting your crops at the right time is essential to get the most out of your greenhouse gardening efforts. With these tips and tricks, you can enjoy a successful and sustainable gardening experience that will nourish you and the planet for years to come.

Your Plan

1. Choose the best fruits and vegetables to plant in your greenhouse.

2. Plant seeds using a direct sow method or in seedling trays.

3. Water your seedlings regularly and make sure they get plenty of sunlight.

4. Prune growing plants as needed and harvest fruits and vegetables when they are ripe.

5. Enjoy fresh, homegrown fruits and vegetables all season long!

CHAPTER 4

USING SUSTAINABLE GARDENING STRATEGIES TO GROW MORE FOOD.

Living in a world increasingly concerned with sustainability and reducing our environmental impact, maintaining a greenhouse garden has taken on new importance. Whether you want to grow more food for your family or take advantage of the fresh produce and beautiful flowers greenhouses offer, sustainable gardening strategies are essential for success.

In this chapter, we will explore four key strategies for sustainable greenhouse gardening: square-foot gardening, crop rotation, hydroponics, and succession planning. Each method offers unique benefits for maximizing yields, minimizing maintenance requirements, and ensuring that your garden is as eco-friendly as possible. These strategies are for you if you are ready to grow more food and enjoy all the benefits of greenhouse gardening. So let's get started!

Square-Foot Gardening

If you're looking to maximize the space in your greenhouse, then square-foot gardening is an excellent method to implement. Square-foot gardening, or SFG, is a strategy for growing plants in a raised bed divided into 1-foot squares. While traditional row planting can be easy, it doesn't make the most of your space. With square-foot gardening, you can grow more fruits and vegetables in less space because of how you arrange your plants.

Using this approach, you calculate the optimal number of plants that can fit into one square foot based on size. For example, you can place one large cabbage head in one square foot while planting 12 carrots in another square foot.

To make a square-foot garden, you will need the following:

1. A raised bed. The bed should be at least 1 foot (30 cm) high so you can reach the plants easily.

2. Soil. Use the best gardening soil you can buy. Your soil should be rich in organic nutrients with excellent water-retaining properties. Sterile gardening soil is preferred, which you can mix with some compost for added nutrients.

3. A grid. The grid will help you keep your plants spaced evenly.

4. Seeds or seedlings.

To plant your square-foot garden, place your plants in the holes created by the grid. Water regularly and fertilize as needed.

Keep your square-foot beds at least six inches deep and a maximum of a foot deep. Your plants should have enough space to be exposed to rich soil nutrients while providing good drainage.

Advantages of Square-Foot Gardening

The benefits of square-foot gardens are many; some include there is less weeding because space is used more efficiently; because of their compactness, the gardens are easier to care for plants yield better in tight spaces; and these gardens warm up faster in the spring, allowing for an earlier harvest.

Setting Up Your Square-Foot Garden

Have you ever wondered just how many plants can thrive in one square foot of a greenhouse? Well, here's your answer! You'll quickly get an idea of what is possible from this list of the most beloved greenhouses plants. So take a few minutes to explore these amazing flowers and herbs that may even inspire some ideas for planting in your own greenhouse.

Vegetable Type	Plant Spacing Per Square	Vegetable Type	Plant Spacing Per Square
Arugula	4	Oregano	1
Asian Greens	4	Parsley	4
Basil	2 to 4	Parsnips	9
Beans (bush)	4-9	Peanuts	1
Beets	9	Peas	4-9
Bok Choy (baby)	9	Peppers (Bell)	1
Broccoli	1	Peppers (All Others)	1
Brussel Sprout	1	Potatoes	4
Cabbage	1	Pumpkins	Two squares per plant
Cantaloupe	2 squares per plant	Quinoa	4
Carrots	9 to 16	Radicchio	2
Cauliflower	1	Radishes	12 to 16
Celery	4	Rhubarb	1
Celtuce	2	Romaine	4
Chives	4	Rosemary	1
Cilantro	1-9	Rutabagas	4
Collards	1	Sage	1
Corn	4	Scallions	36
Cucumbers	2	Shallots	4
Eggplant	1	Sorrel	2
Endive	4	Spinach	9
Fennel	4	Squash	1
French Sorrel	4 to 9	Strawberry	1-4
Garlic	9	Swiss Chard	4
Green Onions	16	Tarragon	1
Kale	1	Tomatoes	1
Kohlrabi	4	Turnips	9
Leeks	9	Thyme	4
Lettuce (leaf)	6	Wasabi	1
Lettuce (sm. head/bibb)	3	Watercress	1
Lettuce (head)	2	Watermelon	Two squares per plant
Melons	Two squares per plant	Yams	4
Mint	1 to 4	Yellow Onion (large)	2-4
Onions (bunching)	9	Zucchini	1

Crop Rotation

Farmers have practiced crop rotation for centuries. This involves growing different crops in different areas of your garden each year. Crop rotation helps to prevent disease and pests from becoming a problem in your garden. It also helps to improve the quality of your soil over time and ensures a good harvest while entirely using the gardening area.

You may wonder, why rotate crops at all? Crop rotation is an eco-friendly method that lessens the incidence of weeds, pests, and diseases while improving the nutrient content and fertility of the soil. We reduce the need for artificial soil amendments and fertilizers and enjoy continuous growing and harvesting seasons. Crop rotation is best applied in greenhouses with raised beds.

Crop rotation is a preventive method for pest and disease control. Different plants attract different pests. When a plant is grown in the same plot of ground, the pest and disease that thrive on the plant become entrenched in the soil and surrounding area. A greenhouse is especially vulnerable to pests and disease because it is a closed system. By rotating plants grown, you prevent pests and diseases from establishing themselves in your greenhouse.

Crop rotation is vital to soil health and fertility. When plants are grown in your greenhouse, they take nutrients out of the soil to produce fruits and vegetables. Greenhouse gardeners face the constant challenge of replenishing the soil. This is often done through synthetic fertilizers and soil amendments. An eco-friendly method of replenishment is rotating the plants that you grow. Crop rotations allow you to replenish the soil consistently by planting a different plant.

Make Your Own Crop Rotation Plan

Crop rotation in a greenhouse takes planning. We are limited by space. If you have several raised beds or are directly sowing, your crop rotation plan will be simple. If you have only one or two raised beds or are container gardening, your plan will take more thought.

I suggest you use a system with a four-part crop rotation plan with crops grouped according to their essential nutritional requirements. Our system will use these groups:

- The Leaf Group that requires nitrogen

- The Fruit Group that needs phosphorus

- The Root Group that relies on potassium

- The Legume Group that deposits nitrogen into the soil

When you look at the rotation, it begins with the legume group, which provides and deposits nitrogen into the soil. The legume group is followed by the leaf group, which requires nitrogen-rich soil. After the leaf group is the fruit group because too much nitrogen can prevent these plants from producing fruit. The root group is next because these plants need potassium. Then the cycle starts again.

The Leaf Group – The Nitrogen-Loving Plants

Nitrogen is a water-soluble nutrient that can easily wash out of the soil. You must plant the leaf group immediately after the legumes, which deposit nitrogen into the soil.

As the name suggests, some of the best crops you can grow are leafy plants like broccoli, cabbage, cauliflower, chard, lettuce, salad greens, spinach, and herbs.

The Fruit Group – The Plants that Need Phosphorus

Some vegetables like cucumber, eggplant, melon, pepper, squash, and tomato are actually considered fruits. This is because they need an adequate supply of phosphorus to bear fruit.

Fruit plants take up a lot of space, so place and space them according to their expected mature sizes.

The Root Group – The Potassium-Reliant Crops

Crops like beet, carrots, garlic, onion, radish, sweet potato, and turnip fall under this group. They require little nitrogen but a lot of potassium.

While potatoes are root crops, they are under the nightshade family, like eggplants, peppers, and tomatoes. Growing potatoes with other root vegetables create a perfect environment for potato beetles. To avoid this, I grow my potatoes with the legume group.

The Legume Group – The Nitrogen-Depositing Plants

This group covers plants like beans, lentils, peas, peanuts, soybeans, and other legume cover crops. They pull nitrogen from the air and store it in their roots, depositing the much-needed nutrient into the ground.

Grow legumes in an open, airy soil environment and allow their roots to decompose in the soil after their season. Doing so deposits more nitrogen into the ground.

Checking Your Soil

Before implementing your crop rotation system, test the soil of your entire garden area. Even if you are starting with fresh soil from the garden store, you should start with fertile soil for your plants. I also suggest you test your soil after one complete rotation through the cycle. This allows you to amend your soil as necessary, depending on its nutrient content. Here are some of the best eco-friendly soil amendments based on the nutritional content of your soil:

- Nitrogen from composted manure
- Phosphorus from bone meal or rock phosphate
- Potassium from greensand
- Lime that can also adjust your soil's pH level

Greenhouses and Crop Rotations- Special Considerations

Crop rotations were developed on farms, so special considerations must be addressed when implementing them in greenhouses. One constraint is determining the plants you want to grow. Often we built a greenhouse to grow our favorite fruits and veggies. Proper crop rotation requires us to grow foods from each category. That may not always be possible. This is often because of the second constraint, space. You may need more space to grow each crop group. The goal is to practice crop rotation as closely as possible for maximum sustainability. You may even consider growing new foods in crop groups you may not have considered before to give your soil a needed replenishment. An ounce of prevention is worth a pound of the cure.

Hydroponics

Hydroponics is an innovative approach to cultivating plants without needing conventional soil. Most systems use a nutrient-rich water solution constantly pumped and redistributed into the roots of plants. Though most systems use water as the growing medium, you can find systems that use sand, fiberglass, and clay balls to grow plants.

Advantages of Using Hydroponics

The hydroponic system is popular for a lot of reasons. It is an eco-friendly method of gardening. Growing fruits and vegetables in a hydroponic system require fewer resources than traditional gardening, making it a sustainable gardening practice. The hydroponic system eliminates the need for harmful pesticides that contaminate our earth by eliminating soil. Lastly, the water used in the system can be recycled, allowing for the wise use of limited water resources. Gardeners who grow plants using this method have been boasting about its benefits for years. Some advantages of raising plants utilizing this approach are:

Improved Water Efficiency: Hydroponics redistributes water through a system that encourages optimal nutrient absorption for the roots. Unlike traditional garden watering systems, hydroponics does not have nutrient runoff as the soil does. This lessens operating costs while preventing unwanted chemicals from contaminating and leaching into local water supplies.

Maximized Space: The compact nature of a hydroponic system makes this method highly efficient and space-saving. A hydroponic system may allow you to grow more fruits and vegetables if you have a small greenhouse.

Reduced Incidence of Pests and Diseases: Soil can contain various pests and diseases that can damage or kill your plants. Hydroponic systems eliminate soil-borne pests and diseases, allowing you to focus on creating the perfect environment for your plants to thrive.

No Need to Weed: Weeds can compete for the nutrients in the soil. However, weeds have difficulty taking root and growing in the water in a hydroponic system. With this method, you can focus on your plants' needs and less time weeding.

Grow More Plants: Not only can you grow more plants in a smaller space, but those plants also produce more than in traditional gardening. Some plants can be very picky about their soil. You can cultivate more hydroponics plants than in soil, and it's easier to grow a wide range of fruits and vegetables with this method.

Year-Round Farming: Hydroponic is another method to extend your growing season. It gives you even great control of the growing environment than just a greenhouse alone. Given you get to control the nutrient levels, ventilation, humidity, and other growth factors, you can maintain the ideal growing environment despite the change of seasons outside. This is especially an advantage for gardeners living in areas where they experience cold winters.

Bigger and More Reliable Harvests: By nature, a hydroponic system is more controlled and provides fewer risks of losing crops due to pests or diseases. Thus, your plants will likely produce bigger harvests due to the ideal growing environment.

Cost-Efficient and Convenient: A hydroponic system allows you to automate your gardening, reducing the time, effort, and costs associated with maintaining your plants in contrast to traditional soil gardens. Thus, you save money and have more time.

Though there are many benefits to hydroponics, there are some disadvantages. A hydroponic system is a costly investment. A medium-sized system can cost several hundred dollars. The systems can be challenging to set up and require constant monitoring and adjustment. If something goes wrong with the system, plants can die quickly.

Succession Planning

You may have heard of succession planting, but what is it? Succession planting is the process of staggering plantings in which crops are planted at different times throughout the seasons. This planting has many advantages, including more fruits and vegetables throughout the seasons, maximized space, extended growing seasons, and minimal losses due to pests, diseases, and poor weather. But most importantly, it is an eco-friendly gardening strategy.

As a gardener, one of the most important things is getting the most out of my plants. I want to maximize my yield so I can enjoy fresh fruits and vegetables all season. That's why succession planting is such an excellent method; it allows me to get the most out of my space and my plants. I can stagger my plantings by succession planting, so I have a continuous supply of fresh produce all season long. Not only do I enjoy fresh fruits and vegetables all season long, but I also minimize any losses due to pests, diseases, or poor weather conditions.

There are three main types of succession planting: staggered planting of the same crop, different crops in the same space, and companion planting.

Staggered Plantings of the Same Crop

The first type of succession planting is called staggered planting when you plant the same crop at different intervals throughout the season. This ensures you have a continuous supply of your produce throughout the season instead of all at once. For example, if you want fresh tomatoes from June through September, you will stagger your plantings so that tomatoes ripen at different times throughout those months.

Different Plants Grown in the Same Space

The second type is called interplanting. Interplanting is when you plant different crops in the same space throughout the season. This type is excellent for small spaces because you can use every inch of your garden! You can also choose complementary plants that will benefit from each other's companionship. For example, snap peas and radishes are a great combination because snap peas climb radishes, which saves space, and radishes deter pests from snap peas. Another example is pairing cabbage with tomatoes because cabbage deters tomato hornworms.

Intercropping

The third type is called intercropping when you plant two or more crops together that will benefit each other. Often called companion planting, it can attract beneficial insects, deter pests, or improve yields. For example, basil deters tomato hornworms and enhances the flavor of tomatoes. Another example is marigolds that deter nematodes and improve the flavor of onions. We will explore this strategy more in the next chapter.

Succession planting is a great way to get the most out of your garden space and plants. By staggering your plantings, you can enjoy a continuous supply of fresh produce all season long. Succession planting should be at the top of your list if you want to maximize your harvest!

Pro Tips

- Avoid planting in the same area if the previous crops encountered pests or diseases.

- Don't be afraid to pull out plants when they are beyond their productive stage. You can place these into your compost bin for future soil amendments.

- Pick varieties that easily and quickly mature to allow you to grow more and harvest more quickly.

The Takeaway

The content in Chapter 4 of Greenhouse Gardening for a Sustainable Future highlights the importance of using sustainable gardening strategies to grow more food in your greenhouse. These strategies include square-foot gardening, crop rotation, hydroponics, and succession planning, which can help you maximize yields and minimize waste while maintaining an eco-friendly approach to greenhouse gardening. Whether you are just starting with greenhouse gardening or are looking to add new techniques to your existing practices, these strategies can help you achieve greater sustainability and self-sufficiency in your garden. We can work together towards a brighter future for our planet and our communities by embracing a more sustainable approach to greenhouse gardening.

Take Action

1. Analyze your current gardening practices to identify areas where you can make changes to become more sustainable. This might include examining your soil quality, conducting regular crop rotations, or incorporating hydroponic systems into your garden.

2. Set goals for how much food you want to grow each season and plan using succession planting techniques. Consider alternating different plants in the same space over time to maximize productivity and minimize waste.

3. Join a local community garden or connect with other local gardeners to share ideas and support each other's efforts. Tap into the wealth of knowledge available in your area and learn from others already successfully incorporating sustainable gardening strategies into their own gardens.

4. Attend workshops or online webinars on square-foot gardening, crop rotation, hydroponics, and succession planting. Gaining hands-on experience with these techniques will help you become more confident in your ability to grow a bountiful harvest using sustainable methods.

5. Commit to yourself and your garden to practice these strategies every season and continuously seek new ways to optimize your yields while minimizing environmental impacts. With a bit of planning, care, and effort, you can create a vibrant and sustainable greenhouse garden that provides abundant food for years to come.

CHAPTER 5

COMPANION PLANTING FOR A BOUNTIFUL GREENHOUSE HARVEST

Native Americans were some of the first to figure out how to use companion planting to grow their crops. Companion planting is a technique where you pair plants together with complementary needs to help each other grow better. This technique produces healthy, productive plants that are easy to take care of.

Coined "the Three Sisters," Native Americans grew corn, pole beans, and squash. Together, these three plants created a beneficial growing environment. Here is how each plant contributed:

- The corn grows tall stalks providing support to the beans.

- The beans draw nitrogen from the air and deposit it into the soil, benefitting the corn and squash.

- With its prickly leaves, the squash keeps away pests and vermin while keeping the soil from drying out too quickly.

  - Additionally, the bean plants grow through squash vines and corn stalks, holding all plants together.

I love growing plants that mutually benefit each other. While you may not want to grow the Three Sisters, you can use this companion planting method for your greenhouse.

In this chapter of Greenhouse Gardening for a Sustainable Future, we explore the many benefits of companion planting – the practice of cultivating certain plants together for mutual benefit. We look at how companion planting works, with tips on which flowers, herbs, and spices are best suited for your vegetable or fruit crops. We also discuss ways to attract beneficial pollinators like bees and butterflies to your greenhouse, helping your plants thrive while contributing to the health of our global ecosystem. Whether you're just starting with greenhouse gardening or looking to incorporate more sustainable practices into your growing routine, this chapter has everything you need to implement this powerful practice.

Why Companion Planting Works

Companion planting is popular for a reason: it works. Let's explore the many reasons why and how companion planting works.

Provides Pest-Repelling and Disease-Suppressing Qualities

Certain plants contain natural pest-repelling or disease-suppressing substances that can help protect their neighboring plants from infestation or infection. For example, garlic is known for its ability to repel aphids, whitefly, and other garden pests. Likewise, marigolds release a chemical into the soil that inhibits the growth of many common root diseases.

Fixes Nitrogen

Some plants, like peas and beans, can fix nitrogen from the atmosphere into the soil. This process makes nitrogen available to other plants, which helps them grow healthier and stronger. Plants from the legume family are notable for their unique ability to draw nitrogen from the air and process it as an organic plant fertilizer.

Legume plants process the nitrogen from the air using their roots that house Rhizobium bacteria. These bacteria can turn the nitrogen in the air into a form that plants can absorb.

Some of the best nitrogen-fixing companion plants are

Acacia (wattle tree)	Clover	Lablab	Peas
Austral indigo	Cowpeas	Lucerne (alfalfa)	Trefoil
Beans	Fenugreek	Lupins	Vetch

Acts as Pest Decoys

Some companion plants are used as diversion crops to draw pests away from the plant that needs to be protected. This method is called trap cropping, where the crops are sacrificed to keep your main plants healthy from infestations.

Dead-end trap crops take this concept further by attracting and killing pests. Two such plants are the Barbarea vulgaris, commonly known as the land cress, and the Barbarea verna, the American upland cress. These plants attract butterflies and moths to lay eggs on the plant. Once the caterpillars eat their leaves, they die.

By planting these decoy crops around the perimeter of your garden, you can effectively keep pests out!

Masks Scents

Most pests instinctively seek their targeted food sources by using scents carried on the wind as identifiers. Companion plants release scents that repel pests while masking and protecting neighboring plants from possible infestations. For example, basil releases a fragrance that deters many common crop pests, including whiteflies and mosquitoes.

When planted near tomatoes, basil helps keep whiteflies away.

Some of the best companion plants that do this include:

Lavender	Scented geranium	Thyme
Rosemary	Southernwood	Wormwood

Provides Visual Masking and Camouflage

Aside from masking scents, some plants can also provide visual masking and camouflage that helps deter pests. For example, hairy vegetables like lettuce are less attractive to leafrollers than smooth vegetables like cabbage. Meanwhile, light-colored vegetables like cauliflower are less attractive to aphids than dark-colored vegetables like Brussels sprouts. By planting these varieties near each other, you can create a barrier that confuses and deters pests.

Creates Protective Environments by Stacking

Another way to deter pests is by stacking different crops on top of each other in a single bed. For example, you could plant tall crops like corn in a bed with shorter crops like lettuce around the perimeter. This stacked arrangement creates an environment where pests have difficulty finding their way to their target crops. Additionally, taller crops can provide shade and shelter for shorter crops from harsh weather conditions.

Acts as Nurse Crops

One of the most exciting things about companion planting is that it can actually help weaker plants thrive. This is because some plants act as "nurse crops," providing support and protection for their weaker neighbors. For example, tall plants like corn or sunflowers can provide shade for delicate plants like lettuce or spinach, helping them to stay cool and prevent them from drying out. Similarly, dense ground covers like clover can help prevent erosion and protect against extreme temperature fluctuations.

Serves as a Habitat for Beneficial Insects and Other Fauna

Another great reason to try companion planting is that it can provide a habitat for beneficial insects and other fauna. This is especially helpful if you're trying to attract pollinators like bees or butterflies to your garden. Certain plants produce nectar or pollen that these creatures are looking for, while others provide shelter from the elements or predators. By creating a diverse habitat with various plant types, you're more likely to attract a broader range of helpful critters to your garden. Plants like calendula, carrot, dill, parsley, and sweet alyssum are planted for this purpose.

Encourages Biodiversity

Finally, companion planting is a great way to encourage biodiversity in your garden. Biodiversity is important because it helps create a healthy ecosystem that can better withstand pests, diseases, and other challenges. Additionally, biodiverse gardens are more beautiful to look at! By planting various species side-by-side, you'll create a colorful and fascinating tapestry sure to draw admiring glances from your friends and neighbors.

Best Companion Plants for Your Vegetables

Due to the infinite number of companion plant combinations, we will cover some of the most common ones and those that should not be planted with each other.

Vegetables you can include are:

Plant	Good Companion Plants	Keep Away From
Lettuce	Beets, radish, carrots, chives, parsnips, garlic, onions, strawberry, tansy, cucumbers	Brassicas (cabbage family)
Onions	Beets, tomato, Brassicas (cabbage family), summer savory, carrot, tansy, chamomile, chard, strawberry, lettuce, parsnips, pigweed, pepper	Beans, peas
Parsnips	Onions, wormwood, radishes	Carrots, fennel, dill, celery
Pea	Beans, turnip, carrots, tansy, chives, corn, radish, cucumbers, mint, early-harvest potatoes	Shallots, garlic, leeks, onions
Potatoes	Basil, beans, celery, corn, garlic, horseradish, lettuce, marigolds, onions, peas, radishes, spinach	Asparagus, tomatoes, broccoli, strawberries, Brussels sprouts, sunflowers, cabbage, squash, cauliflower, raspberries, carrots, peppers, cucumbers, melons, eggplant, kohlrabi
Pumpkin	Beans, squash, marigolds, corn, nasturtiums	Potatoes
Radishes	Beets, squash, cabbage, spinach, carrots, lettuce, chives, kale, cucumbers	Hyssops
Spinach	Brassicas (cabbage family), eggplant, strawberries, celery, Fava bean, cauliflower	Hyssop
Squash	Beans, radishes, corn, sunflowers, dill, marigolds, nasturtiums, strawberries, peas	Potatoes

Plant	Good Companion Plants	Keep Away From
Lettuce	Beets, radish, carrots, chives, parsnips, garlic, onions, strawberry, tansy, cucumbers	Brassicas (cabbage family)
Onions	Beets, tomato, Brassicas (cabbage family), summer savory, carrot, tansy, chamomile, chard, strawberry, lettuce, parsnips, pigweed, pepper	Beans, peas
Parsnips	Onions, wormwood, radishes	Carrots, fennel, dill, celery
Pea	Beans, turnip, carrots, tansy, chives, corn, radish, cucumbers, mint, early-harvest potatoes	Shallots, garlic, leeks, onions
Potatoes	Basil, beans, celery, corn, garlic, horseradish, lettuce, marigolds, onions, peas, radishes, spinach	Asparagus, tomatoes, broccoli, strawberries, Brussels sprouts, sunflowers, cabbage, squash, cauliflower, raspberries, carrots, peppers, cucumbers, melons, eggplant, kohlrabi
Pumpkin	Beans, squash, marigolds, corn, nasturtiums	Potatoes
Radishes	Beets, squash, cabbage, spinach, carrots, lettuce, chives, kale, cucumbers	Hyssops
Spinach	Brassicas (cabbage family), eggplant, strawberries, celery, Fava bean, cauliflower	Hyssop
Squash	Beans, radishes, corn, sunflowers, dill, marigolds, nasturtiums, strawberries, peas	Potatoes
Sweet Potato	Okra, peppers, sunflower	Sorghum, Johnson grass
Zucchini	Beans, spinach, corn, radishes, dill, peas, garlic, marigolds, oregano, nasturtiums	Potatoes, pumpkin

Best Companion Plants for Your Fruits

If you are growing fruit bushes or trees, here are some of the best companion plants for them:

Plant	Good Companion Plants	Keep Away From
Apple	Chives, southernwood, garlic, marigolds, clover, comfrey, nasturtium, daffodils, leeks, foxgloves	Carrots, potatoes, eggplant, tomatoes, cedar, walnut
Apricot	Alliums (cultivated onion, garlic, scallion, shallot, leek, chives), basil, buckwheat, comfrey, nasturtiums, peaches, plums, southernwood, tansy	Barley, oats, wheat, peppers, potatoes, tomatoes, eggplant, sage
Banana	Beans, sweet potato, comfrey, papaya, nasturtiums, legumes and peas	
Blackberries	Grapes, tansy	Raspberries, since blackberries will take over the raspberries
Blueberries	Clover, yarrow, strawberries	Tomatoes
Citrus	Alfalfa, thyme, borage, parsley, clover, nasturtium, comfrey, marigold, dill, lemon balm, hyssop, lavender	Avoid plants prone to mildew and other fungal diseases
Cucumber	Beans, tomato, Brassicas (cabbage family), corn, tansy, early-harvest potatoes, sunflowers, English pea, oregano, nasturtium, radish, marigold	Potato, sage
Fruit Trees	Place fruit trees in tandem with at least two together. Their best companions are alliums, tansy, borage, mustards, comfrey, marjoram, daffodils, marigold, dandelions, nasturtiums, lemon balm	Avoid plants prone to mildew and other fungal infections.
Grapes	Basil, oregano, beans, mulberry, clover, hyssop, elm trees, geraniums	
Melon	Chamomile, summer savory, corn, squash, nasturtium, radish, oregano, pumpkin	
Papaya	Banana, sweet potato, beans, nasturtiums, comfrey	

Passion fruit	Beets, Swiss chard, carrots, strawberries, eggplants, spinach, potatoes, leeks, onions, lettuce	Corn, sweet potato, cowpea, sorghum, okra
Peaches	Asparagus, tansy, borage, southernwood, basil, onion, comfrey, garlic	Grass, tomato, raspberries, potato
Pear	Aromatics, nasturtium, comfrey	Grass, potato, tomato, raspberries
Peppers	Basil, tomato, carrots, tansy, clover, parsley, eggplant, onions, marjoram	Brassicas (Cabbage family), kohlrabi, fennel
Strawberries	Borage, thyme, bush beans, spinach, cabbage, Pyrethrum, caraway, onion, lettuce	Brassicas (cabbage family), potato
Tomatoes	Asparagus, tansy, basil, stinging nettles, bee balm, sage, borage, Brassicas (cabbage family), rosemary, carrots, pepper, celery, parsley, chives, onion, dill (until mature), nasturtium, gooseberries, mustard, marigold, mint	Corn, kohlrabi, potatoes, fennel, pole beans, walnuts, mature dill
Watermelon	Marigold, nasturtium	Mustard, potato

Flavor and Scent with Companion Herbs and Spices

Now that you know you can place herbs as companion plants, here are some of our favorites:

Herbs	Why We Love Them
Basil	Improves the growth of neighboring plants, repels mosquitoes, and helps tomatoes taste better.
Chives	The perfect companion to carrots by improving growth and flavor. Keep away from beans and peas.
Cilantro	This is an ideal companion for beans, peas, spinach, and tomato by attracting beneficial insects like hoverflies, parasitoid wasps, and tachinid flies while repelling aphids, spider mites, and potato beetles.
Dill	Plant near cabbage to improve growth and overall health. Keep away from carrots and tomatoes since it attracts tomato hornworms.
Fennel	Fennel inhibits growth, causes bolting, and may kill many garden plants.
Garlic	Plant near raspberries to repel Japanese beetle.
Horseradish	Plant at each corner of your potato patch to discourage potato bugs.
Lavender	Grow this plant near cabbage and cauliflower since it is a natural repellent of aphids, fleas, moths, slugs, and ticks. Remember that it needs full sun despite little water and almost no fertilizer. Place it near plants with similar growing needs.
Mint	Perfect companion plant for cabbage and tomatoes by improving their health and flavors. Peppermint specifically repels white cabbage moths while spearmint discourages ants and aphids.
Rosemary	Grow next to beans, cabbages, carrots, and sage since it deters cabbage moths, bean beetles, and carrot flies. Keep away from basil.
Sage	Grow this with cabbage, beans, carrots, and even rosemary since it deters cabbage moths, bean beetles, and carrot flies. Avoid planting near cucumbers.
Tarragon	Plant throughout the garden since its scent highly discourages most pests while enhancing the growth and flavor of crops grown with it.
Thyme	You can plant this companion in spots all over your garden. Ideal companion plant for cabbages since it deters cabbage worms.

Flowers for Your Food and Food for Pollinators

Like open fields, greenhouses will also need pollination. You will need to attract pollinators into your greenhouse, especially if you grow fruits like tomatoes. If you've ever opened your greenhouse to find that your tomatoes have stopped growing or your cucumbers have failed to produce fruit, it's likely because there wasn't enough pollination. Thankfully, there are a few strategies you can utilize to encourage pollinators into your greenhouse so that your plants have the best opportunity to flourish! By encouraging beneficial insects, like bees, into your greenhouse, you help your plants produce fruits. Here are a couple of strategies to make sure you invite the pollinators into your greenhouse

Open Your Greenhouse

It seems counterintuitive. We build a greenhouse to have more control over our plant's environment, so opening the doors may seem a little troublesome. But bees and butterflies cannot get in if we keep the door closed. Draw in pollinating species like bees and butterflies by opening your greenhouse doors to allow some extra warmth inside.

Plant Pollinator-Attracting Plants

Some plants, like lavender and echinacea, are naturally attracted to pollinators. By planting these plants in your greenhouse, you're giving the pollinators a reason to come in.

Stop Using Insecticides and Pesticides

Many insecticides and pesticides are harmful to bees and other pollinators, so it's important to avoid using them if you want to attract them into your space. Instead of using toxic chemicals to repel pests, use companion plants that repel pests, attract pest predators, or mask the scent or visual display of your plants.

Add Some Flowers

Pollinating insects like bees are attracted to the bright petals of flowers since these signal nectar. If you have space available, consider planting native wildflowers in a garden around your greenhouse. The native flowers and plants will attract pollinators to your greenhouse. If you are limited in space, add a couple of containers of wildflowers near the greenhouse door.

Here are some excellent flowering companion plants you can grow:

Flowering Companion Plants	Why We and the Bees Love Them
Borage (Borago officinalis)	Borage flowers attract a lot of bees, which delight many gardeners. You can even eat its leaves and flowers, which come with a subtle cucumber flavor. This fast-growing and self-reseeding plant can be directly sown in the ground.
Pot Marigold (Calendula officinalis)	Calendula, or pot marigolds, are part of the daisy family and are edible with a strong bitter flavor. Calendula discourages pests, such as asparagus beetles and tomato hornworms, but it also attracts others, like aphids. Use the flower as a trap crop by placing it away from plants that aphids attack.
Cosmos (Cosmos bipinnatus)	Cosmos attract many helpful insects, such as green lacewings, due to their white or bright orange petals. Green lacewings eat up soft-bodied insects, such as aphids, scales, and thrips.
Marigold (Tagetes sp.)	Marigolds deter pests both above and below the ground while being attractive. Mexican bean beetles will be discouraged by planting marigolds with bean plants. Marigolds have also repelled squash bugs, thrips, tomato hornworms, and whiteflies. Some marigolds contain specific chemicals that kill root nematodes found in the ground.

Nasturtium (Tropaeolum majus)	Nasturtiums repel beetles and squash bugs while being great trap crops for aphids. Nasturtium flowers are also edible, and you can keep the seeds for planting in the next season, although most nasturtiums will self-seed.
Sunflower (Helianthus annuus)	Grow sunflowers as fantastic trellis structures for climbing plants. Sunflowers also have a lot of nectar that attracts pollinators. Plant a coarse-leaved vegetable, such as squash, under the sunflower to deter animals like the occasional squirrel.
Sweet Pea (Lathyrus odoratus)	Grow sweet peas with peas and pole beans to attract bees. Take note that sweet peas will not cross-pollinate with edible peas because they are in different families.
Zinnia (Zinnia elegans)	Zinnia flowers attract bees and hummingbirds with their rich supply of nectar. You can also use the pastel-flowered varieties as trap crops to attract Japanese beetles if you have crops suffering from this pest. Even better, cut flowers make wonderful flower arrangements.

The Takeaway

As we have seen throughout this book, greenhouse gardening is essential for sustainable living, providing us with fresh and healthy food free from harmful chemicals. By incorporating companion planting into your greenhouse practices, you can enhance the beauty and productivity of your plants while also attracting pollinators that help support a thriving ecosystem. Whether you are growing vegetables, fruits, herbs, and spices, there are many companion plants suited to each type of plant that can help make your greenhouse more sustainable through increased growth and decreased need for pesticides or other chemicals. With these simple tips and tricks, anyone can succeed in their greenhouse garden, creating a more sustainable future for themselves and generations to come.

Take Action

1. Experiment with different companion planting combinations to find the best matches for your specific climate and growing conditions.

2. Keep a detailed record of which plants seem to thrive together and any challenges or successes you encounter along the way.

3. Consider incorporating various flowering plants into your greenhouse garden to attract pollinators and add beauty and fragrance to the space.

4. Pay close attention to how different herbs and spices can be combined with your fruits and vegetables, not only for flavor but also for their potential health benefits and medicinal properties.

5. Remember that supporting biodiversity is an important part of sustainable greenhouse gardening, so do what you can to create habitats that will encourage wildlife, such as bees and butterflies, to visit your garden.

CHAPTER 6

THE DARK SIDE: SOIL HEALTH IN GREENHOUSE

One of the most important aspects of greenhouse gardening is soil health. The health of your soil directly affects the health of your plants. Healthy soil is rich in nutrients and microorganisms essential for plant growth. It also has good drainage so that excess water can drain away from the roots of your plants. This chapter will discuss why soil health is vital for greenhouse gardening and how you can maintain healthy soil.

Why Is Soil Health Important?

The quality of your soil directly affects the quality of your plants. Plants need nutrients and microorganisms to grow, which are found in healthy soil. Healthy soil also has good drainage, which helps excess water drain away from plant roots. Poorly-drained soils can lead to "damping off," a condition in which seedlings rot at the base or young plants wilt and die.

Healthy soil is full of life. Healthy soil is teeming with bacteria and fungi (known as mycorrhiza). These microbes are essential in breaking down organic matter and making nutrients available to plants.

One reason why soil health is so essential for greenhouse gardening is that greenhouse plants require more water than those in a garden. This means that the soil in your greenhouse is constantly being replenished with water, which can leach nutrients out of the soil and make it harder for plants to access those nutrients. This is why it's so important to have a healthy level of microbes in your greenhouse soil; they help to break down organic matter and make nutrients more readily available to plants.

Understanding your Soil

Soil is the medium by which our plants get moisture and nutrients. By learning the composition of the soil, we can quickly determine how to amend it, so it is ready for planting.

A good soil test will help you arrive at three things: the basic structure of your soil, the pH level, and the available nutrients. Utilizing your soil test results, you can effortlessly adjust and balance your soil to cultivate a thriving environment for your plants.

Ideally, soil tests should be run every three to five years to determine its pH level and nutrient content. Soil testing can be done any time of the year, although the most preferred time is autumn. Testing during the fall gives you time to correct any imbalances and prepare the soil for winter and spring planting.

There are three ways to do soil testing. The first option is to get a commercial home test kit for soil at gardening centers. The kit is easy to use, although it is less thorough and accurate thanas a professional test taken at a local county extension office, which is the second option. Regional county extension offices usually charge a small amount to test the soil, while some even offer the service for free. The third option is to test your soil yourself using homemade materials.

How To Take a Soil Test

1. Go to an area of your outdoor space and clear away surface litter and plant residue. Your sample area should be clear of any ashes, burned materials, manure, or compost.

2. Use a trowel or shovel to cut straight into the soil. The cut should be at a depth of six to eight inches with a V-shaped hole.

3. Take out your trowel with six or eight inches of soil. Cut away its width until the soil sample is about one inch wide and six or eight inches long.

4. Place the content in a clean bucket or glass jar. To sample more than one area, you can use the steps above and mix the samples.

5. Allow the soil to dry out indoors for several days before you test your soil.

Understanding Your Soil Test Results

Depending on the method of your soil test, you will most likely have these results that show the following nutrient amount or recommendation found in your soil:

Normally, three elements will be shown: nitrogen, phosphorus, and potassium. Together, they form the acronym N-P-K.

Nitrogen (N) is an essential soil component that helps plants produce healthy leaves. Nitrogen can come from fresh or dried manure, bloodmeal, and even vegetable-based meals from alfalfa, cottonseed, and soybean.

Phosphorus (P) helps in your plants' germination, root health, flowering, and fruiting requirements. Phosphorus helps plants absorb minerals, assists in robust growth, and withstand diseases. Bone meal and bone char provide ready sources of phosphorus, while rock phosphates deliver this component on a slow but long-term basis.

Potassium (K) or potash regulates water flow in plant cells, which helps with your plants' overall growth, flowering, fruiting, and disease-resistant characteristics. Greensand, granite dust, and wood ash are high in potassium content.

3 Do-It-Yourself Soil Tests

This handy DIY soil test will help you determine the following soil conditions:

- Soil-type structure through the peanut butter jar test

- pH test using baking soda and vinegar to determine the acidity or alkalinity

- Nutrient level by using the earthworm test

The Peanut Butter Jar Test

Ideally, healthy soils comprise 40 percent sand, 40 percent silt, and 20 percent clay. This test will take about an hour to set up and needs a whole day to finish. You will use these materials:

- Sample soil

- Glass jar with a straight flat side similar to a peanut butter jar or mason jar

- Ruler

- Timer

Find an empty glass jar with a straight flat side. You can use most peanut butter or mason jars. The jar should have a lid. Place the sample soil you want to test inside the jar. Ensure your sample soil fills the glass jar about a third to a half-jar full.

Pour water into the jar until the water reaches the shoulder of the jar. Allow the soil to soak up the water before you put on the lid. Twist the cap until the jar is tightly closed, and shake the glass jar hard for about three minutes.

Set the glass jar down and count down to one minute.

Measure the sediment that has accumulated at the bottom of your jar with a ruler after one minute. This is the sand found in your sample soil.

Wait four more minutes and measure the sediment in the glass jar again. The difference between this measurement and the previous one is the silt in your soil.

Allow the glass jar to remain undisturbed for 24 hours before you measure the sediment. The difference between the third and second measurements shows the clay found in your soil.

Now, check how your measurements compare with the ideal percentage of the soil. For example, if your total sediment is 10 inches, the perfect soil should have 4 inches of sand, 4 inches of silt, and 2 inches of clay.

Based on your results, you will better understand if your soil has too much or too little sand, silt, or clay.

Using the peanut butter jar test, you can amend your soil to adjust to your plants' growing needs.

The Pantry Soil pH Test for Soil Acidity or Alkalinity

For this test on soil pH, you will need the following:

- Two tablespoons of sample soil
- 2 glass or plastic bowls
- 1/2 cup of vinegar
- 1/2 cup of baking soda
- 1 cup of distilled water

Take two tablespoons of your sample soil and place them inside a bowl. Add your half cup of vinegar. If the soil fizzes up with the added vinegar, that means your soil is alkaline.

Take another two tablespoons of your soil sample. Place them inside a bowl and moisten the soil with distilled water. Add in your half cup of baking soda. If the soil fizzes up, then your soil is acidic.

If there is no reaction, your soil has a neutral pH level, which is ideal for most plants. A neutral sits somewhere within the 5.5 to 7 range. This condition allows plant roots to absorb nutrients optimally due to good microbial activity in the soil.

To balance soil that is too acidic, you can add a bit of finely ground limestone for optimal results. To counteract overly alkaline soil, add some ground sulfur.

The Earthworm Test

This test will work if you're not squeamish about earthworms. You might need to ask someone to do this for you if you are. Earthworms are an indication of the soil's nutrient content. The more earthworms in your soil, the healthier it is. The best time to do this test is during the spring when the soil temperature is moist and around 50 F.

To check for the earthworm population in your soil, dig up about one cubic foot of soil. Break up the soil and look for earthworms. Healthy soils have at least ten earthworms per cubic foot. If you end up with less than 10, add more organic matter to your soil, such as compost, leaf mold, and aged manure. Organic matter improves the structure while releasing nutrients and increasing microbial activity in the soil.

Soil Amendments

You can amend the soil with the ingredients you have around the house. Here are some of my favorite organic amendments to soil:

- Unlock the power of nitrogen in your soil by utilizing used coffee grounds! Reusing them is an easy and effective way to boost your plants' nutrients. However, ensure they've cooled completely before applying them; if hot coffee grounds are added, they could damage your plants!

- Eggshells: Eggshells are a great source of calcium carbonate, which helps regulate pH levels in the soil. They can also deter slugs and snails (crush them up and sprinkle them around the base of your plants).

- Compost: Compost is full of essential nutrients like nitrogen, phosphorus, and potassium that plants need to grow. You can make it yourself by recycling your kitchen scraps, or you can buy it at most nursery or garden stores.

- Wood Ashes: Wood ashes contain potassium and other minerals that can benefit plant growth. Be careful to use only a little, as wood ashes can raise the pH level of your soil if used in excess.

- Banana peels: Utilizing banana peels for your plants is an excellent way to promote their growth. Rich in phosphorus and potassium, two vital nutrients for flourishing vegetation, simply burying the peel whole near the base of your plant or chopping it into smaller bits will do wonders!

- Epsom salt: Epsom salt is rich in magnesium sulfate, which helps improve flower blooming and seed germination. It's also great for deterring slugs! Sprinkle Epsom salt around the perimeter of your garden bed or directly on problem areas.

Composting: The Ideal Soil Amendment

When most people think of composting, they think of gross, rotting food scraps. But believe it or not, composting is a fantastic way to improve soil quality and make your garden thrive! Composting is taking all of your organic waste - like vegetable peels, fruit skins, coffee grounds, etc. - and putting it in a bin or container to decompose. The result is a dark, earthy material that can be added to your garden soil to help it retain water and nutrients.

The Benefits of Making Your Compost

Aside from being cost-efficient, making your compost is the easiest way to improve the health of your soil. It can help us achieve optimal soil health without harming our immediate environment. The benefits of composting include the following:

Increased Microorganisms in the Soil

Compost is teeming with a host of beneficial microorganisms, such as fungi and good bacteria, which work to aerate the soil by decomposing organic matter. They also prevent pathogens from developing and increasing. The number of microbes and macronutrients in compost help plants produce robust root systems.

Amended Soil Texture and Improved Nutrient Content

Instead of yearly soil tilling, compost helps to transform hard-packed soil into loose earth. Compost is especially beneficial for sandy soils as it helps to hold in moisture for the roots to absorb. It contributes to the soil's nitrogen, phosphorus, and potassium content while adding micronutrients. Since it is organic matter, these nutrients get released slowly over an extended period.

Reduced Chemical Runoff

Compost is organically charged with nutrients, eliminating the need for commercial chemical fertilizers. Commercial chemical fertilizers dispense nutrients into the ground more quickly than compost. These chemicals enter the waterways and sewer systems, affecting the immediate aquatic and marine ecosystems.

Decreased Landfill Waste

Biodegradable food waste can be diverted from landfills and used as compost materials. By making our own compost, we lessen the household waste and materials otherwise sent to landfills. In landfills, nutrients found in organic compost will go to waste.

Compost Methods

There are three main types of composting: direct composting, open-air composting, and tumbler composting. Let's take a closer look at each one.

Open-Air Composting

Let's start with the most basic composting method: open-air composting. Open-air composting is precisely what it sounds like—it simply involves creating a pile of organic matter (leaves, grass clippings, fruit and vegetable scraps, eggshells, coffee grounds, etc.) and letting it decompose over time.

Open-air composting offers many advantages, not least of which is its affordability! You don't need to purchase any elaborate machinery or components – all you require is an isolated corner in your garden where the waste can remain undisturbed.

Another benefit of open-air composting is that it's easy to add material to your pile as you generate it. Have some kitchen scraps? Just toss them on the pile! You don't need to worry about storing them in a bin until the bin is full.

However, there are also some downsides to open-air composting. One is that your pile can attract animals if it is not adequately covered. Another is that the process can take longer than other methods—it can sometimes take up to two years for a traditional compost pile to fully decompose.

Direct Composting

If you want to expedite the composting process, try direct composting! Direct composting involves placing organic matter directly into your garden bed instead of creating a separate compost pile.

One benefit of direct composting is that it's quick—you don't have to wait for your material to decompose before using it in your garden. Chop up your kitchen scraps and dig them into the soil!

Another benefit of direct composting is that it enriches your soil immediately. Since the organic matter goes directly into your garden bed, there's no waiting period before your plants can benefit from its nutrients. If you use this method, chop your organic material into small pieces. This will speed up the rate of decomposition.

Tumbler Composting

If you're short on space or worried about attracting animals, a compost tumbler might be a good option. Compost tumblers are sealed bins that tumble as they rotate, aerating the contents and speeding up the decomposition process.

By opting for a compost tumbler, you can reap several benefits—including an unprecedented level of cleanliness. With the bin firmly sealed shut, there's no risk of any animals being drawn in or your material spilling onto the ground.

Tumblers are also compact and perfect for small yards or patios. With their fast-acting decomposition process, using them is the ideal solution for quickly producing nutrient-dense soil for your garden.

Tumblers have some drawbacks, however. They can be expensive, ranging from $100-$200 depending on their size and features. They also require more effort than other methods—you must regularly tumble the bin to maintain aeration and speed up decomposition.

Components of a Good Compost

There are four things you need to make compost aside from the system of your choice. These things are air, water, nitrogen materials, and carbon materials. Below is a list of brown and green materials you can use for your compost. Aim for an equal amount of the two.

Green Matter	Brown Matter
Animal manures from chicken, cow, horse, rabbit, sheep except dog or cat manure	Bark, twigs, and chipped tree branches
Annual plants and weeds that have not set seed	Corn stalks
Coffee grounds	Plain corrugated cardboard
Eggshells	Dried hedge trimmings and prunings
Fruit and vegetable peels and scraps	Fall leaves, hay, straw, sawdust
Grass clippings	Paper from newspaper, napkins, writing paper, paper towels, printing paper, paper plates, and coffee filters
Seaweed	Pet bedding
Tea leaves, teabags with the tags removed	Pine needles
Fresh trimmings from healthy perennial and annual plants	Plain brown paper bags
Wood ash but not too much	Pure cotton fabric

Do not add the following to your compost:

- Autumn leaves

- Citrus, which is slow to rot and very acidic, reducing worm activity

- Cat and dog manure

- Coal fire ash
- Coated or glossy paper
- Coffee bags
- Color-printed paper
- Cooked food
- Dairy products
- Diseased plants
- Labels on vegetables and fruits
- Large branches
- Onions
- Perennial weeds
- Raw meat
- Scraps from fish and meats
- Synthetic fertilizer
- Tea bags
- Treated wood sawdust

Whether it's budget, space limitations, or the need for nutrient-rich soil to be added to your garden, various home composting approaches have their advantages and disadvantages. Knowing which approach works best for you will depend on your specific requirements.

Open-air composting might be right for you if you have plenty of space and patience. However, if you're short on time or space, consider investing in a compost tumbler.

Regardless of your chosen method, remember that composting is a critical way to reduce our reliance on fossil fuels and help our environment!

Takeaway

As more people turn towards greenhouse gardening to increase their self-sufficiency and sustainability, we must take steps to protect the soil health in our greenhouses. This involves understanding your soil and taking measures to improve its quality through techniques like testing, amending, and composting. With these simple steps, you can help ensure a healthy and productive greenhouse for years to come.

Take Action

1. Perform a soil test to determine your soil's composition and nutrient levels and take appropriate steps to correct any imbalances or deficiencies.

2. Incorporate compost into your planter beds to improve their overall health and help them retain moisture more effectively.

3. Use organic fertilizers and pest management methods like crop rotation and companion planting to keep your soil vibrant and healthy.

4. Consider building a compost bin to create your own source of organic fertilizer for your greenhouse plants.

5. Consult with an expert or do additional research on best practices for maintaining healthy soil in a greenhouse setting and make adjustments over time.

Chapter 7

Pest, Disease, and Sanitation Management for Greenhouse Gardeners

Once I started my greenhouse gardening journey, I remember being so excited when my tomatoes turned red. I knew I was only a few weeks away from a bountiful harvest. The next time I walked into my greenhouse, I found my tomatoes with holes in them! Something was eating my tomatoes before I could. I was devastated! At that moment, I wanted to find the most potent chemical available and kill those bugs! I didn't, but it was a struggle.

An ounce of prevention is worth a pound of cure, but gardening often requires both. This chapter will explore how to prevent and treat greenhouse gardens' most common pests, diseases, and viruses. You will learn how to take care of your gardening tools and equipment so they are free of anything that would infect your plants. I hope you can use this information to reap the benefits of your first harvest.

Pest Control the Natural Way

Since we aim to go organic, we should also look into controlling and repelling pests naturally; it's best to inspect your plants regularly to identify and treat pests before they become fully blown-out infestations.

Aside from companion planting, here are great ideas to incorporate into your gardening.

Predator Insects

One natural pest control method is introducing predator insects into your garden. Ladybugs, for example, love to eat aphids. Green lacewings will devour whiteflies, mites, and small caterpillars. And praying mantises will gobble up about any other crawling insect. You can purchase these beneficial insects online or at your local nursery. Release them into your garden and let them do their thing!

Concentrated Plant Extracts and Oils

You can use certain plant extracts and oils for natural pest control. Garlic oil, for instance, is an effective repellent for many insects, including aphids, Japanese beetles, and root maggots. Cedar oil can keep ticks, fleas, and mosquitoes at bay. And diluted milk has been shown to deter aphids from attacking plants. You can make your own insecticidal spray by mixing these ingredients with water and a dash of dish soap. Be sure to test it on a small plant area first to ensure it causes no damage. Also, research any plant extracts and oils because beneficial insects may be affected when you use these.

Neem Oil

Neem oil is an excellent insect repellant because it suffocates pests. Pests do not eat the leaves sprayed with neem oil nor lay eggs on a treated plant. You can make your own insecticide with it. First, mix water and neem oil using a ratio of about one tablespoon per gallon of water. After thoroughly mixing the solution, pour it into a spray bottle and liberally apply it to your plants and any place where pests may be present. The neem oil will kill any bugs that come into contact with it, but it's important to note it will only kill the bugs with which it comes into direct contact. It won't keep them from returning (that's why you need to reapply it every few days), but it's still an effective way to get rid of pests.

If you're dealing with a critical pest infestation, adding dish soap to your solution (around one teaspoon per gallon of water) will ensure the neem oil is spread evenly and sticks firmly on surfaces. Be wary, though; too much detergent may harm your plants.

Nematodes

Nematodes are tiny parasitic worms that feed on harmful garden pests like cutworms, grubs, and flea larvae. They're totally harmless to humans, pets, and beneficial insects but deadly to the pests they target. You can purchase nematodes online or at your local garden center. Mix them with water according to the package directions and water them into the soil around your plants. Remember, nematodes do not prevent pests but only seek to eat them.

Organic Dishwashing Liquid

You can add a diluted solution of organic dishwashing liquid to spray black and green flies. This solution usually kills them on contact. It is best to spray this solution more than once daily and for a few days apart.

Pro Tip

- While screens protect against pests, they prevent beneficial insects and pollinators from visiting our plants.

Identifying and Treating Common Pests

Below are six common greenhouse garden pests and proven ways to treat them.

Aphids

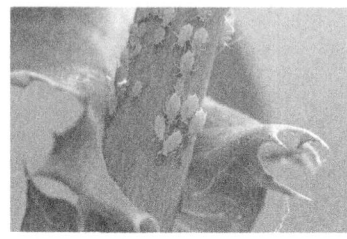

Aphids are tiny yet formidable pests that can wreak havoc on your garden if left unchecked. These sap-sucking bugs have an insatiable appetite for plant matter and can quickly cause severe damage to the flora in your yard. They come in various colors, but they're usually green or black. Aphids can be incredibly destructive as they ravage both indoor and outdoor plants, often congregating in great numbers on the undersides of leaves. If you have aphids in your garden, you'll notice leaf curling, yellowing, and stunted growth. You may also see ants crawling around, as they're attracted to the honeydew produced by aphids.

Try blasting them away with your garden hose for a swift solution to aphids! If you're looking for something more long-term, insecticidal soap and neem oil are effective options to keep your garden free from these pesky pests!

Fungus Gnats

Fungus gnats are tiny black insects attracted to damp soil. They're common in houseplants and potted plants but can also be found in outdoor gardens. These pests feed on plant roots and fungi, damaging your plants and making them more susceptible to disease. If you have fungus gnats, you may notice poor plant growth, discolored leaves, wilting, and root rot.

You can try using yellow sticky traps or nematodes to eliminate fungus gnats. You can also let the top inch of your soil dry out between watering to make it less attractive to these pests. Ensure that your water sources are covered and that there is no excess or standing water on the ground. Refrain from overwatering your plants

Whiteflies

Whiteflies are winged insects that feed on the sap extracted from plants, coating them with honeydew and creating an ideal environment for sooty mold to grow. Not only do they pose a nuisance due to their presence, but also as they attract ants whose behavior can further damage your plants. Whiteflies are especially fond of tomato plants, but they also infest potatoes, squash, beans, cucumbers, okra, eggplant, sweet potatoes, peppers, melons, citrus fruits, Hibiscus flowers, and impatiens.

To get rid of whiteflies naturally, you can try using whitefly traps or releasing beneficial insects such as lacewings or ladybugs into your garden. You can also use an insecticide such as neem oil.

Spider Mites

Despite their minuscule size, spider mites are a significant pest to many plants as they feed on the juices within. These destructive insects belong to the same family of spiders and ticks and can be found in nearly every corner of our planet. Spider mites get their name from their two pairs of legs (most insects have three pairs of legs). They range from red to green to brown and are barely visible to the naked eye. Adult spider mites are about the size of a grain of salt.

Spider mites can wreak havoc on your garden by feeding off the leaves of beloved plants, transforming their lush green hue to a sickly yellow or brown. Heavy infestations can cause leaves to drop off altogether. In addition to causing damage to plants, spider mites can also spread diseases from one plant to another.

Exterminating Spider Mites can be a difficult process. Start by removing infested leaves. Dispose of infested leaves in sealed bags so the spider mites can't escape and reinfest your plants. Introduce predators - several predatory insects will happily feast on spider mites, including ladybugs, lacewings, and pirate bugs.

The most effective way to address spider mites is by taking proactive steps and avoiding them altogether! Keep an eye out for early signs of infestation and act immediately if you see anything suspicious. In addition, make sure your plants are well cared for, as stressed-out plants are more likely to attract spider mites.

Thrips

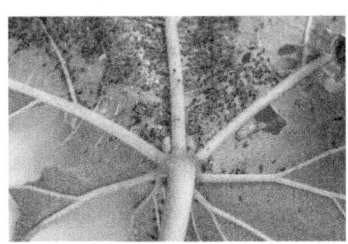

Thrips are tiny, winged insects that measure just 1/25 inch long. They range from light yellow to black and have two pairs of long, slender wings. Thrips feed by puncturing plants and sucking out the juices, which can cause stunted growth, deformities, and discoloration. They are especially fond of roses, but they will also attack a wide variety of other plants, including tomatoes, peppers, beans, cucumbers, squash, zucchini, eggplant, potatoes, impatiens, petunias, marigolds, and zinnias. Thrips are most active in late spring and early summer.

Thrips suck out the chlorophyll in plants, leaving them unable to photosynthesize correctly, resulting in plant and flower deformities. Look for leaf discoloration or stippling (tiny dark spots), deformities (such as curling or distortion), or stunted growth.

Several solutions are available if you want to get rid of thrips. You can handpick them off your plants – This is only effective if you have a few plants with a light infestation. You can use insecticidal soap – This method is effective but will need to be repeated every few days until the infestation is under control. You can use neem oil or introduce beneficial predators – Lacewings and pirate bugs are both effective predators of thrips.

The Dangers of Fungus, Bacterial Diseases, and Viruses

Our plants are like us, susceptible to disease. Fungi, bacteria, and viruses are some of the most common infections that target plants. Greenhouses go a long way in helping gardeners keep their plants healthy. However, the same safe environment can also be detrimental when infected by unwanted diseases. In this chapter, we will explore the world of plant diseases, learning prevention strategies, as well as how to cure them and keep your garden healthy.

Fungi

Fungal pathogens cause approximately 85 percent of plant diseases, spreading through water, soil, and air. Contaminated tools, such as unwashed or unsterilized pruning shears, also contribute significantly to the spread.

Some of the most common fungal diseases are:

Black Spot

Dark patches will appear on the top sides of the leaves. As the fungus develops, it expands until the leaves are mostly yellow and filled with black spots. Black spot is caused by water remaining too long on the surfaces of plants. The fungus reproduces even more quickly during long periods of heavy rainfall and is exacerbated by restricted airflow and humid conditions.

Rust

Found on the underside of leaves, rust is a collection of vibrant orange bumps that make the leaves look like they are rusting. The infected leaves become yellow and discolored as the fungus develops before eventually falling off. Constant wetness and humidity encourage the fungi to reproduce, which are further spread by water droplets, wind, and insects.

Botrytis Blight

Also known as gray mold, Botrytis blight impacts plants through their bulbs, buds, flowers, and leaves. Infected plants are often covered with a smattering of gray mold after a long period of cool, damp weather. Parts of the plant will grow deformed and irregular, the most obvious being the flowers and leaves.

Powdery Mildew

Multiple fungi can show up as powdery mildew on various plants. White or light gray powdery spots are signs of infected leaves, stems, flowers, and fruit. Powdery mildew can even grow on vegetables. The most susceptible part of the plant is the new growth. Leaves turn yellow, deformed, or wilted.

Root Rot

When various fungi in the soil are encouraged to grow in constant and overly wet conditions, they attack the root system. Wet soil is often a result of gardeners mistaking wilted plants for being dehydrated. They give the plants more water, fueling fungal growth and causing them to exhibit yellow or wilted leaves, leaf drops, or stunted growth.

Organic Fungicides and Prevention:

Many fungicides on the market claim to be organic. But with so many products on the market, it takes time to know which one is right for you. To make the most informed decision on which organic fungicide would best suit your garden, let's consider three of the top options - sulfur, copper, and horticultural oil. By comparing their respective benefits and drawbacks, you can select one that works ideally for you!

Sulfur

Gardeners have been using sulfur for centuries, making it one of the most trusted and widely used fungicides available today. Sulfur powder is inexpensive, easy to find, and effective against a wide range of fungi, including powdery mildew and black spot. One benefit of sulfur is that it can be used as both a preventive measure and a treatment; regular dusting your plants with sulfur powder will help keep fungal infections at bay. However, if your plants are already showing signs of infection, you must apply a heavier dose of sulfur to treat the problem. Please be careful when using sulfur, as an excessive amount can be detrimental to the health of your plants.

Sulfur can also be an insecticide; when combined with lime, it effectively treats aphids, mites, and other common garden pests.

Copper

Copper is another popular choice for gardeners looking for an organic fungicide. Like sulfur, copper is relatively inexpensive and easy to find; you can usually find it at your local hardware store or nursery. Copper sulfate and copper hydroxide are the two most common forms of copper fungicide. They are both highly effective against a wide range of fungi, including powdery mildew, black spot, downy mildew, and early blight. Copper fungicides are also effective against bacteria and some viruses.

One thing to remember with copper fungicides is that they can be toxic to plants if used in high concentrations. They can also stain concrete or stone surfaces, so use them with caution around sensitive areas. When applied correctly, however, copper fungicides are safe for humans and animals and will not harm your plants.

Horticultural Oil

Horticultural oil is a broad-spectrum fungicide effective against various fungi, including powdery mildew, black spot, rusts, scale insects, aphids, mites, whiteflies, and mealybugs. Horticultural oil works by suffocating the fungus or insect; however, because it works by physical contact rather than chemical contact like other fungicides on this list) it must come into direct contact with the fungus or insect to be effective. This means horticultural oil must be applied more often than other fungicides to keep your garden healthy.

Horticultural oils are safe for people and animals when used as directed; however, they can sometimes cause leaf burn if applied in direct sunlight or when temperatures are high. It is absolutely essential that you read the labeling and follow the instructions before using horticultural oil in your garden.

Use these other tips to control or prevent fungal infections:

- Practice good garden hygiene and sanitation by removing and destroying all infected plants upon detection.

- Dispose of all infected parts safely to prevent spread. Do not add them to your compost pile.

- Space out your plants properly to avoid damp and humid conditions; this promotes healthy airflow and regulates humidity and ventilation simultaneously.

- When pruning, ensure your tools and clothing are cleaned and sterilized before and after.

- If a plant is infected, pause any fertilization because the fungi quickly attack new growth.

- Water the soil instead of watering overhead to avoid wetting the leaves and flowers, thus reducing the risk of fungal growth.

- Use sterile, well-draining soil.

- Quarantine new plants before transplanting them into your garden or greenhouse.

Alternative Homemade Anti-fungal Solutions

If you prefer a gentler alternative to fungicides, you can use homemade remedies against fungal infections. So that you know, these homemade solutions work best only when the infection is still in the early stages. If the condition is more severe, you may have to look for more robust options, such as fungicides explored previously.

These home remedies need frequent application to treat the infections completely. Spray mixtures need to be applied liberally because they only kill what they come into contact with.

Here are some of the best homemade anti-fungal recipes that work well:

Neem Oil Solution

This recipe calls for a one-gallon mixture. You can adjust your ratio accordingly depending on the number of plants that need to be sprayed.

- Pour two tablespoons of neem oil into a bottle and add one tablespoon of organic liquid soap. Do not use detergent. Close the bottle and shake the mixture well to emulsify both ingredients.

- Slowly add the neem oil and liquid soap solution to a gallon of water until everything is mixed well. Use this water to spray all your infected plants.

Use the neem oil and liquid soap solution immediately, or its potency will be significantly reduced.

Potassium Bicarba onate

Gardeners use this as an organic fungicide to effectively treat black spot, mildew, and Botrytis.

- In a one-gallon water container, mix in one tablespoon of potassium bicarbonate and half a teaspoon of mild liquid soap. Avoid using detergents.

-

Mix well until everything is combined perfectly.

- Use the mixture for all infected plants and apply it liberally.

Baking Soda (Sodium Bicarbonate)

This all-purpose product works well in reducing fungal infections.

- Mix one tablespoon of baking soda with half a teaspoon of organic liquid soap.
- Pour this solution into a gallon of water.
- Use this solution to spray liberally on infected plants.

I find this more effective as a preventative measure on plants adjacent to or near the infected ones.

Onions and Garlic

Onions and garlic can be a fungicide.

- Peel and chop four to five large onions and place them inside a large container.
- Pour 10 to 12 liters of boiling water into the container and allow the mixture to sit for 6 to 10 hours.
- Use the mixture as an anti-fungal spray on all affected and unaffected leaves.

Milk

Canadian researchers discovered milk spray solutions effectively prevented fungal infections in barley and tomato over 50 years ago. This solution faded in popularity with the advent of chemical fungicides.

Recent movements that encourage organic gardening have revived this method. Gardeners have rediscovered milk as an effective natural fungicide.

- Mix one part milk with two or three parts water.
- Use as a spray solution. Spray on infected leaves and other plant parts liberally.

Bacterial Control and Prevention

Bacterial infections are hard to treat, so prevention is always your best course of action. To avoid harmful bacteria, keep these tips in mind:

- Immediately remove identified infected plants and dispose of them safely. Do not place them in compost.

- Purchase and plant bacteria-resistant varieties, cultivars, and hybrids.

- Make sure your propagation materials are free from bacterial contamination.

- Disinfect and sterilize all your tools, clothing, and equipment.

- Look into crop rotation to reduce the risk of bacteria overwintering in the soil, affecting plants for the next growing season.

- Prevent, clean, and disinfect plant surface wounds to prevent bacterial entry into the tissue.

- Practice proper spacing and ventilation for your plants.

- Locate your plants in their most appropriate growing areas.

- Prevent or repel pests to limit infestations.

- Make sure your soil is sterile and clean.

- Quarantine new plants before final planting.

- Bacterial infection can be treated using chemical applications, such as antibiotics and copper-containing compounds.

Viruses

Plant-feeding insects are some of the usual suspects in spreading harmful plant viruses in the garden. Viruses need to be physically carried to contaminate other plants. Virus infection is incurable, and infected plants must be swiftly identified and destroyed. Viruses can live in garden soil for years. Symptoms are varied, but the most common ones include discolored yellow rings on leaves. Some viruses also leave white, yellow, or pale green mosaic patterns. Other symptoms include stunted and deformed growths from abnormally narrow, swollen, puckered, or rolled-up leaves. Some common viruses are:

- Citrus Tristeza- This causes citrus trees to slowly decline in health before their eventual death. This virus is spread mainly through aphids.

- Tomato Spotted Wilt- Brown or yellow rings on tomato leaves or fruits signify this virus. It also causes wilting and asymmetrical or lopsided growth on watermelons, peppers, and other plants.

- Cucumber Mosaic-Affecting cucumbers, celery, cantaloupes, squash, tomatoes, and occasionally peppers, this virus can range from mild to severe. Symptoms include subtle mosaic patterns on leaves and stunted deformed growth.

Unfortunately, no chemical treatments exist to eliminate virus infections in plants. Your best option is to identify, eliminate, and dispose of all infected plants properly and safely.

Sanitation for Greenhouses

I must admit that cleaning is my least favorite chore in the greenhouse. But I learned the hard way to set aside time each year to do a deep clean. I enjoyed my greenhouse for quite a few years before my windows were cloudy. When I looked closer, I found algae growing on the glass. Yuck! As I looked in corners and moved benches, I found a lot of moss and dirt in places typically hidden by plants. It was time for a deep clean. Over the years, I made it a habit to give my garden a deep clean once a year. I live in the north, so I deep-clean my greenhouse in October before it gets very cold. Fewer gardening tasks exist, leaving ample time to deep clean my greenhouse.

In this section, I will share my tips on cleaning your greenhouse and taking care of your tools and equipment.

Cleaning Your Greenhouse

When I say deep-clean, I mean deep-clean. Remove everything in your greenhouse and give it a good cleaning. You may need to find a safe place for any plants or seedlings that may still be growing in your greenhouse. Pick a warm day to move your plant to protect plants from the weather.

Here are my best tips and techniques for cleaning your greenhouse:

- Take your plants out of the greenhouse. Before you take them out, inspect each one carefully for pests or diseases.

- Take all pots, tools, equipment, and other items out of the greenhouse. Again, carefully inspect each one.

- Clean your greenhouse from top to bottom. Starting at the top ensures that any dirt, pathogens, or eggs will fall first before you clean the lower portions of your greenhouse.

- If there were any plants with pests or diseases, segregate the trash and dispose of it properly and safely. Do not place contaminated items into your compost.

- Do an initial scrub of all surfaces with large pieces of moss, algae, and other unusual growths. Sweep and collect these in a separate pile of trash and dispose of the trash correctly.

- Get a bucket and fill it with warm water. Use mild liquid soap or dishwashing liquid.

- Scrub all surfaces, starting at the top, and then work your way down. Use brushes of several sizes, including toothbrushes, to help clean surfaces, nooks, and crannies.

- Rinse the scrubbed surfaces with clean water.

- Begin scrubbing the floor with the same warm soapy solution and rinse after.

- Allow everything to dry.

- Once everything is dry, go over everything with a homemade vinegar spray to naturally disinfect the surfaces. Vinegar also gives glass that extra sparkle.

It would be best if you cleaned the exterior of your greenhouse before cleaning out the interior. Ensure that you clean the drains where algae can grow.

To help you further, here's a checklist for deep-cleaning the exterior of your greenhouse:

- Sweep away all debris, including leaves and moss, from your greenhouse's sides, roof, and gutters.

- Use brushes and scrapers with medium and long handles to get to hard-to-reach places. Use a ladder if necessary.

- Use your tools to scrape off all visible moss as much as possible.

- Use mild soapy water to reduce chemical reactions to the materials of your greenhouse.

- Don't forget to deep clean the water butts and adjoining structures, such as downspouts and gutters. Use a long-handled broom with a rag wrapped around its end.

- As much as possible, use products with eco-friendly ingredients to reduce harm to plant and animal life. Anti-bacterial soap solutions are harmful because they can encourage any remaining bacteria to build resistance and become harder to eliminate.

- Use isopropyl alcohol or hydrogen peroxide instead. Remember:

  - 70 percent isopropyl alcohol is ideal for disinfecting tools but can irritate your skin or respiratory system. Use in a well-ventilated area.

  - Hydrogen peroxide is also an excellent product for disinfecting tools.

Tips on Cleaning Your Gardening Tools

Gardening tools should also be deep-cleaned. In addition to deep cleaning once a year, make it a habit to keep your gardening tools regularly cleaned and sanitized to keep them well-maintained and prevent contamination from pests and diseases.

I recommended using these techniques when cleaning, maintaining, and storing your gardening tools:

- Blast away the mud, dirt, and grime with your garden hose. Focus on hitting the ends of the tools you use the most.

- Fill a five-gallon bucket with hot water.

- To clean your tools, mix a tablespoon of dish soap into the water and let them soak for half an hour.

- Rinse and dry your tools with a rag or cloth to reduce rusting or spotting.

- Scrape any hardened materials with a scraper, putty knife, or stiff wire brush.

- If you cannot scrape away the materials, apply a mixture of baking soda paste. It is non-toxic and more effective. You can use one part baking soda to one part water or adjust as necessary. Baking soda can also remove rust.

- Sanitize your tools using vinegar. Use vinegar at full strength or dilute it to half-strength with water. You can even add salt to the vinegar to help remove rust.

- Take caution when using vinegar because it can kill plants and grasses.

- Sharpen your tools, especially those you use for digging, pruning, and cutting.

- To sharpen your tools, wipe the edge of your tools with some vegetable oil.

- Take a flat metal file and work the file at a shallow angle until you get the sharpness you desire.

- Wipe down all tools with an oiled cloth to eliminate metal filings that can dull your blades.

- Tighten up all the bolts, nuts, and screws.

- Wipe down your tools with an oiled cloth to prevent rust. Include any wooden handles to keep them well-lubricated.

- Drop lubricating oil on all moving parts, such as pivots and hinges.

- Remember to clean and disinfect your tools' cabinet or storage area.

- If you can hang long-handled tools, so they don't get deformed.

- Smaller tools will do well in a bucket full of sand with vegetable oil to keep them oiled from rust.

Remember, regular cleaning and maintenance can help prolong your tools' life.

Take Away

As you can see, many natural methods exis for taking care of pests in your greenhouse and keeping your plants healthy. Whether it's using predator insects, concentrated plant extracts or oils, nematodes, or simply cleaning the greenhouse and garden tools regularly, you can keep your plants thriving without harming the planet or yourself with toxic chemicals. Use these tips today to help create a sustainable, healthy future for yourself and the world!

Take Action

1. Identify the most common pests in your greenhouse and use this book to research natural ways to control them.

2. Practice good sanitation habits in your greenhouse by regularly cleaning it and your gardening tools.

3. Use organic fungicides and other treatments to prevent bacterial diseases and viruses and take steps to strengthen your plant's immune systems.

4. Experiment with different methods of pest control and sanitation to find what works best for your specific greenhouse environment.

5. Stay up-to-date on the latest research and best practices in greenhouse gardening so you can continue to improve your garden's health and sustainability.

Chapter 8

Greenhouse Gardening In Every Season

Greenhouse gardening is essential to a sustainable future, as it allows us to grow our own fruits and vegetables free from the harmful effects of pesticides. In this chapter, we will explore how to garden in every season, from spring to winter, so that you can enjoy fresh, locally-grown produce year-round. So dive in and start planting today – for a more sustainable tomorrow!

Greenhouse Gardening in the Spring

Revel in the beauty of spring! As you bask in the sunshine and witness gorgeous blossoms, what better time to plan your summer greenhouse garden? To get started, here are a few helpful tips.

Planting Quick-Growing Plants

You can plant the last of your quick-growing cold-weather plants in early spring, like beets, broccoli, and salad greens. These plants don't mind a little cold weather and will be ready to harvest in a few weeks. Towards the end of spring, you can start annual flowers for outside flowerbeds. By planting them in the greenhouse now, you'll give them a head start on the growing season. They'll be ready to plant out in May or June when the weather is warm.

Starting Warmth-Loving Plants

In late spring, when the weather stays warmer, you can start warmth-loving plants like tomatoes, peppers, and eggplants. These seeds require no less than 10 hours of daily sun and temperatures above 60°F (15°C) to sprout. If the required warmth is challenging, you can opt for a heat mat as an effective solution.

Fertilizing Garden Beds

Another important task for early spring is fertilizing your garden beds. This will help ensure that your plants have all the nutrients they need to thrive. In previous chapters, I discussed how to test your soil, so you know how to amend the soil. Also, think about the plants you will grow during the summer months. What nutrients need to be present in the soil for those plants to thrive?

Greenhouse Gardening in the Summer

Grow! Grow! Grow! Here are my top ten picks for summer fruits and vegetables to grow in the greenhouse.

Tomatoes - Tomatoes are one of the most popular vegetables to grow in the greenhouse. They thrive in warm, humid conditions and produce abundant fruits. With numerous tomatoes available to choose from, the possibilities for your greenhouse are endless! Do some research to determine which cultivars will flourish in your particular environment.

Cucumbers - Cucumbers are another excellent choice for the greenhouse. They also thrive in warm, humid conditions and will produce an abundance of fruits. Cucumbers are versatile vegetables used in salads, sandwiches, or even pickled.

Squash - Squash is another excellent option for the greenhouse. There are wide varieties of squash, so you'll find one that suits your taste. Squash is a hearty vegetable perfect for stews and soups.

Eggplants - Eggplants are delicious vegetables that can be grown in the greenhouse. They prefer warm temperatures and need well-drained soil. Eggplants can be used in many dishes, so get creative!

Peppers - Peppers are another fantastic option for the greenhouse. From the fiery reds to the mellow yellows, peppers come in various sizes and colors that will captivate your tastebuds. There's a pepper for everyone! Peppers are versatile vegetables used in salads, salsas, or cooked.

Herbs - Herbs are an excellent addition to any garden and can also be grown in the greenhouse. Herbs prefer warm temperatures and well-drained soil. They make a great addition to salads, soups, sauces, and more.

Watermelons - Nothing says summer like biting into a crisp, juicy watermelon—and luckily, it's easy to grow your own! Look for seedless varieties like 'Sugar Baby' or 'Moon and Stars.' The distinct advantage of these types of watermelon is that they are ideally suited to greenhouses due to their space-saving nature, unlike other varieties.

Cantaloupe - Cantaloupe is another delicious summer fruit that is easy to grow in a greenhouse. Look for varieties like 'Ambrosia,' 'Cream of Saskatchewan,' or 'Hales Best Jumbo.'

Lettuce - Salads wouldn't be the same without lettuce—and fortunately, it's one of the easiest things to grow in a greenhouse! Look for mesclun mixes or pre-packaged mixes specifically designed for growing in greenhouses."

Greenhouse Gardening in the Fall

Autumn is the time to deep clean and resets your greenhouse for the winter growing season. But even during this season, you can grow and harvest vegetables.

Start Seeding the Greenhouse for Winter Production: Late August is the perfect time to start new seeds for a late fall and winter harvest. Crops like kale, arugula, beets, carrots, spinach, broccoli, and Brussels sprouts will all do well in cooler weather. Planting them now will give you a head start on the season and ensure a continuous supply of fresh produce all winter.

Consider crops that can thrive despite the dwindling fall daylight: When the days get shorter, most plants go into dormancy. But still, some crops thrive in this environment. Onion, garlic, and peas are all excellent choices for late-season planting.

Deep Clean the Greenhouse: Before you plant for the fall season, it's essential to give your greenhouse a good cleaning. This will help prevent diseases and pests from taking hold and ruining your crop. Once everything is clean and ready to go, you can prep the soil for planting.

Insulate Against the Cold weather: As winter approaches, you'll want to insulate your greenhouse against the cold weather. This will help keep your plants warm and protect them from damage due to freezing temperatures.

Greenhouse Gardening in the Winter

Building an unheated greenhouse doesn't mean you must put your green thumb to rest during the winter months! Winter temperatures can stimulate the sugar production in some root vegetables, which helps to protect their roots from freezing damage while giving them a delightful boost in sweetness. So don't pack up those gardening tools yet. Here are tips on what vegetables you can grow and how to give them a fighting chance in the cold.

What to Grow

Carrots, beets, radishes, and turnips love the cold and will do well in most winter climates. There is no shortage of leafy greens, either. You can grow kale, lettuce, spinach, arugula, and parsley. If you live in a milder climate (Zone 7 and above), you can also try growing hardy herbs like chives and thyme.

When selecting varieties of these vegetables to grow in the winter, look for cold-tolerant ones. Carefully review the information on the back of your seed packet to understand better when you can anticipate harvesting. It is crucial to growing plants to maturity before the days shorten. With less light, growth will decrease dramatically.

Plant Care in the Winter

You can take specific steps to ensure your garden stays healthy and vibrant during winter. Cold-tolerant plants will survive the cold but will not survive freezing. In unheated greenhouses covering or mulching plants can help boost heat retention in the soil and protect delicate roots from freezing. Gardeners also use a heat sink to keep temperatures above freezing. A heat sink is just a barrel of water in your greenhouse. The water absorbs the heat during the day and slowly releases it at night.

In the summer, you water your plants every day, but in the winter, you must change your practices. As the days get colder, water your plants less. Once the temperature outside is below freezing, I suggest you don't water your plants.

Continue to pay attention to ventilation in your greenhouse. Condensation will quickly occur on your windows due to the temperature differential in your greenhouse compared to outside. Also, avoid using chemical fertilizers before winter planting as they can damage delicate root systems. Instead, choose organic fertilizers that slowly release nutrients throughout the winter months.

Unfortunately, fruits and fruiting vegetables cannot be grown during the winter due to the lack of pollinators. However, there are many beautiful vegetables you can harvest during the winter. As always, careful planning will ensure a bountiful harvest.

The Takeaway

As more people turn to greenhouse gardening to grow their food and live more self-sufficiently, we should focus on eco-friendly solutions to help preserve these vital spaces for future generations. As more people learn of the need to care for our environment and embrace sustainable practices, greenhouse gardening has become an increasingly popular way to grow food year-round. It doesn't matter if you have a heated greenhouse or not. You can grow food year-round.

Conclusion

You are now equipped with all the information you need to build your greenhouse and grow your plants using eco-friendly techniques. The beauty of this process is that everything you create will be tailored specifically to your needs. Before we end this book, let's go through some of the most critical touchpoints you need to remember for greenhouse gardening.

Determining the kind of greenhouse should always be your first move. Look into the various structures available and decide which suits your lifestyle best. Choosing your greenhouse structure for the long haul is essential since you may end up tending to your plants with great enthusiasm!

You can maximize the interior of your greenhouse, so all your staging materials are aligned with your needs. This includes selecting the appropriate benches, shelves, and tables. Try to incorporate vertical planting to optimize the space of your greenhouse. Don't forget to use shade cloth to prevent overheating in your greenhouse.

Once you're ready to start, consider the plants you want to grow. Whether you start your plants as seeds or purchase seedlings, you should give them the proper care. Watering, feeding, pruning, and harvesting your plants should be carefully thought out to make your gardening experience smooth.

Using eco-friendly gardening practices will not only protect the earth from harmful pesticides and commercial fertilizers, but they will also help you increase your yield. Consider square-foot gardening, crop rotation, and succession planning to optimize your planting and harvesting timelines. You might also look into alternative methods of growing your vegetables, such as hydroponics.

Taking care of your plants also means protecting them from pests and diseases. Remember, companion plants help repel pests while inviting beneficial insects to guard and pollinate your plants and may even improve the flavor of your produce.

Soil health is as important as plant selection. This includes looking into what kind of soil you have and what you can do to improve its texture, nutrient content, and overall quality. You can always have your soil checked for a complete assessment and evaluation, or you can conduct DIY soil tests. Both will help you improve your soil condition.

One of the best ways to improve your soil is composting. You can make your own compost instead of purchasing it from garden centers. Making compost is easy as long as you know the basic requirements. Plus, you get to recycle all the food waste you have generated. This benefits the earth and your garden.

Despite your best efforts, pests and diseases still appear in your garden. When this happens, you have many organic options for treating and preventing pests and diseases. To address outbreaks, you can use predator insects like ladybugs or natural substances like sulfur or copper. Take the same approach when treating fungi, bacteria, and viruses.

Keeping a clean greenhouse is also a preventative measure. Your greenhouse should get a deep cleaning yearly, and tools should be cleaned and maintained monthly. If you experience an infestation or infections, you should wash and sanitize your tools daily, as well as any gardening gloves, aprons, or clothing. It helps you avoid contamination and spreading the infestation or infection while setting you up for a better gardening routine.

Another great routine is maintaining your tools to avoid rust, deterioration, and disrepair. Sharpen and lubricate all necessary tools right after disinfecting them; they will last longer.

The beauty of a greenhouse is that you can grow food all year long. That's right, even through the winter. Choose cold, hardy plants to grow during the coldest months of the year. Many root vegetables and greens produce more sugars and are sweeter during the winter. You can overwinter fruit trees in your greenhouse if you live in more temperate areas.

As more people become interested in sustainable living and minimizing their environmental impact, greenhouse gardening has become an increasingly popular way to grow food and enjoy fresh, healthy produce right at home. By using eco-friendly practices in your greenhouse, you will reap a bountiful harvest and rest easy knowing you have done your part in being a good steward of the earth.

Thank you for purchasing my book on greenhouse gardening. It will help you navigate this exciting journey toward self-sustainability and eco-friendliness. If you find any value in this book, please leave me an honest review. Reviews can help me better understand what my readers need and inform other potential buyers.

In addition to the book, I will continue developing more content for greenhouse gardening enthusiasts like yourself. Stay up-to-date on my progress by following me on social media or signing up for my email list.

Keep Growing,

Kacey Collier

Works Cited

"8 Fruit Trees You Can Grow From the Seeds and Pits of Your Own Fruit." *Bright Side Â Inspiration. Creativity. Wonder.*, 22 Sept. 2022, brightside.me/creativity-home/8-fruit-trees-you-can-grow-from-the-seeds-and-pits-of-your-own-fruit-498010.

"8 Methods of Composting." *Direct Compost Solutions*, 22 Sept. 2022, directcompostsolutions.com/8-methods-composting.

8 Ways a Hydroponic Greenhouse Can Save You Money | Rimol Greenhouse. 14 Oct. 2020, www.rimolgreenhouses.com/blog/8-ways-hydroponic-greenhouse-can-save-you-money.

10 Different Types of Greenhouses | Structures and Designs. www.ourendangeredworld.com/eco/types-of-greenhouses.

"15 Basic Greenhouse Pest Control Tips and Tricks." *GreenHouse Planter*, 16 Oct. 2019, greenhouseplanter.com/15-basic-greenhouse-pest-control-tips-and-tricks.

Anderson, Tanya. "Deep Cleaning the Greenhouse With Eco-friendly Products." *Lovely Greens*, 1 Jan. 2021, lovelygreens.com/deep-cleaning-greenhouse-eco-friendly.

Andrei310. "Whitefly Aleyrodes Proletella Agricultural Pest on Cabbage Leaf." *iStock*, www.istockphoto.com/photo/whitefly-aleyrodes-proletella-agricultural-pest-on-cabbage-leaf-gm1405873015-457631037?clarity=false.

Angelo, View All Posts By. "What Is Companion Planting and How Does It Work?" *Deep Green Permaculture*, 19 June 2022, deepgreenpermaculture.com/2009/08/17/companion-planting.

Arcadia GlassHouse. "Tip #12: Sizing Your Greenhouse for Optimum Utilization of Space." *Arcadia GlassHouse*, 31 Mar. 2016, arcadiaglasshouse.com/greenhouse-tips/tip-11-sizing-your-greenhouse-for-optimum-utilization-of-space.

Baker, Libby. "5 Types of Greenhouses You Can Build Out of Recycled Materials." *One Green Planet*, 1 Oct. 2019, www.onegreenplanet.org/lifestyle/types-of-greenhouses-you-can-build-out-of-recycled-materials.

Barnes, Stephen. "Wooden Racks in a Greenhouse With Tomato Plants." *iStock*, www.istockphoto.com/photo/wooden-racks-in-a-greenhouse-with-tomato-plants-gm1427279377-471263610?clarity=false.

BBC Gardeners' World Magazine. "How to Make Compost." *BBC Gardeners World Magazine*, 8 Sept. 2022, www.gardenersworld.com/how-to/maintain-the-garden/how-to-make-compost.

The Best Things You Can Do for Your Garden Soil - Bob Vila. https://www.bobvila.com/slideshow/the-best-things-you-can-do-for-your-garden-soil-52131

Browning, Sara J. "When to Harvest Fruits and Vegetables." *NebGuide*, July 2011, extensionpublications.unl.edu/assets/html/g2089/build/g2089.htm.

Buckner, Heather. "Succession Planting: How to Grow Crops for a Continual Harvest." *Gardener's Path*, 8 Jan. 2022, gardenerspath.com/how-to/hacks/succession-planting.

Carruthers, Daniel. "Greenhouse Tools and Equipment." *Cultivar Extraordinary Greenhouses*, Apr. 2020, www.cultivargreenhouses.co.uk/inspiration/greenhouse-tools-equipment.

Ceres Greenhouse Solutions. *6 Common Greenhouse Pests and How to Manage Them.* 18 May 2021, ceresgs.com/6-common-greenhouse-pests-and-how-to-manage-them.

Coramueller. "Hands Seeding Seed in Garden Soil." *iStock*, www.istockphoto.com/photo/seeding-gm168764343-23987273?clarity=false.

Domnicky. "Group of Earthworms in the Ground and Compost, as Background...." *iStock*, www.istockphoto.com/photo/group-of-earthworms-in-the-ground-and-compost-as-background-gardening-concept-gm1356232264-430459783?clarity=false.

Eremeychuk, Leonid. "Trimming the Tree With a Cutter. Spring Pruning of Fruit Trees." *iStock*, www.istockphoto.com/photo/trimming-tree-with-a-cutter-spring-pruning-of-fruit-trees-gm1136104804-302463868?clarity=false.

Farm Homestead. "Companion Planting Chart for Herbs - Farm Homestead." *Farm Homestead - Healthy Self Reliance*, 21 June 2018, farmhomestead.com/gardening-methods/companion-planting-chart-herbs.

Finn, Jason. "Gothic Arch Greenhouse With Glass Panel and Green Door Below The..." *iStock*, www.istockphoto.com/photo/gothic-arch-greenhouse-with-glass-panel-and-green-door-below-the-stainless-gm1446640581-484667751?clarity=false.

Fruit Companion Plants – Nathalie Strassburg. nathaliestrassburg.com/the-medicine-garden/fruit-companion-plants.

"Getting Started With Greenhouse Ventilation Systems." *Advancing Alternatives*, 23 Oct. 2019, www.advancingalternatives.com/blog/getting-started-greenhouse-ventilation-systems.

Grandbrothers. "A Woman Is Dumping a Small Bin of Kitchen Scraps Into an Outdoor..." *iStock*, www.istockphoto.com/photo/a-woman-is-dumping-a-small-bin-of-kitchen-scraps-into-an-outdoor-tumbling-composter-gm1355559503-430014297?clarity=false.

Grant, Amy. "Greenhouse Location Guide: Learn Where to Put Your Greenhouse." *Gardening Know How*, 11 Feb. 2021, www.gardeningknowhow.com/special/greenhouses/where-to-put-greenhouse.htm.

Grant, Bonnie. "Vegetables for Hanging Baskets: Growing Vegetables in a Hanging Basket." *Gardening Know How*, 21

Apr. 2021, www.gardeningknowhow.com/special/containers/vegetables-for-hanging-baskets.htm.

"Growing Fruit Trees in Pots and Containers." *Henry Street Garden Centre*, 29 July 2021, www.henrystreet.co.uk/growing-fruit-trees-in-pots-containers.

Heft, Todd. "Companion Planting: Flowers, Vegetables, Herbs and Fruit Are Better Together." *Big Blog of Gardening*, 8 Nov. 2022, www.bigblogofgardening.com/companion-planting-flowers-vegetables-herbs-and-fruit-are-better-together.

---. "Companion Planting: Flowers, Vegetables, Herbs and Fruit Are Better Together." *Big Blog of Gardening*, 8 Nov. 2022, www.bigblogofgardening.com/companion-planting-flowers-vegetables-herbs-and-fruit-are-better-together.

How to Choose the Best Greenhouse Materials to Extend Your Gardening Season. insteading.com/blog/greenhouse-materials.

"How to Test Your Garden Soil (and 3 DIY Tests)." *Almanac.com*, www.almanac.com/content/3-simple-diy-soil-tests.

Instructables. "Hydroponics - at Home and for Beginners." *Instructables*, 13 June 2022, www.instructables.com/Hydroponics---at-Home-and-for-Beginners.

"Internal Vs External Shade Cloths for a Greenhouse - What's Better?" *Greenhouse Emporium*, 22 Nov.

2022, greenhouseemporium.com/blogs/greenhouse-gardening/internal-vs-external-shade-cloths-greenhouse.

Jess311. "Scouting for Spider Mite on Tomato Leaves. A Large Population Of..." *iStock*, www.istockphoto.com/photo/scouting-for-spider-mite-gm1268293209-372249800?clarity=false.

Jorruang, Tinnakorn. "Hand Protects Seedlings That Are Growing, Environment Earth Day In..." *iStock*, www.istockphoto.com/photo/hand-protects-seedlings-that-are-growing-environment-earth-day-in-the-hands-of-trees-gm1132646260-300360130?clarity=false.

L., Lesa. "Garden Crop Rotation - a Simple System." *Better Hens & Gardens*, 29 Mar. 2021, www.betterhensandgardens.com/garden-crop-rotation-a-simple-system.

Lenhof, Ren. "Pruning Vegetables: What Plants to Prune and Which Ones Not To." *House Fur*, 23 July 2021, housefur.com/pruning-vegetables-what-plants-to-prune-and-which-ones-not-to.

Leupold, Marc. "Some Dark-winged Fungus Gnats Are Stuck on a Yellow Sticky Trap." *iStock*, www.istockphoto.com/photo/yellow-sticky-trap-in-a-houseplant-pt-gm1285286397-382167780?clarity=false.

LiveWall LLC. "Benefits - LiveWall Vertical Plant Wall System." *LiveWall Green Wall System*, 4 Oct. 2022, livewall.com/benefits.

Lnzyx. "A Kind of Insects Named Aphid on the Green Plant." *iStock*, www.istockphoto.com/photo/aphid-on-the-green-plant-gm178610334-24416769?clarity=false.

Lokakalin, Puripatch. "Photo of Pests, Cotton Aphid, Cotton Bollworm, Pseudococcidae And..." *iStock*, www.istockphoto.com/photo/pests-cotton-aphid-cotton-bollworm-pseudococcidae-and-thrips-palmi-karny-on-a-okra-gm1131818703-299811698?clarity=false.

Ly, Linda. "Marry Your Flowers and Veggies: Companion Planting Guide to Your Garden." *Gilmour*, 10 May 2019, gilmour.com/companion-planting-chart-guide.

M, Ana. "How to Build a Greenhouse Rainwater Catchment System?" *Greenhouse Growing*, 30 May 2020, www.growingreenhouse.com/how-to-build-a-greenhouse-rainwater-catchment-system.

---. "How to Grow Seeds in a Greenhouse? Step-By-Step Guide." *Greenhouse Growing*, 15 Feb. 2020, www.growingreenhouse.com/how-to-grow-seeds-in-a-greenhouse-step-by-step-guide.

---. "Types of Benches in Greenhouse. Shelves, Staging and Bench System." *Greenhouse Growing*, 30 May 2020, www.growingreenhouse.com/types-of-benches-in-greenhouse-shelves-staging-and-bench-system.

Macrovector. "Traditional Lean-to Glass Greenhouse With Young Plants Isometric..." *iS-*

tock, www.istockphoto.com/vector/greenhouse-isometric-composition-gm1201209377-344390262?clarity=false.

Miller, Laura. "How to Plant Fruit Seeds: Tips for Sowing Seeds From Fruit." *Gardening Know How*, 13 Jan. 2022, www.gardeningknowhow.com/edible/fruits/fegen/planting-seeds-from-fruit.htm.

Monk, Joe. "Post Author: Joe Monk." *Greenhouse Info*, 15 May 2022, greenhouseinfo.com/types-greenhouse-flooring.

---. "Post Author: Joe Monk." *Greenhouse Info*, 15 Sept. 2020, greenhouseinfo.com/vertical-gardening-in-greenhouses.

Nolan, Tara. "Direct Seeding: Tips on Sowing Seeds Right in the Garden." *Savvy Gardening*, 16 Apr. 2022, savvygardening.com/direct-seeding.

---. "The Benefits of Composting: Why You Should Use This Valuable Soil Amendment." *Savvy Gardening*, 3 Dec. 2022, savvygardening.com/benefits-of-composting.

Noonan, Jennifer. "The Best Things You Can Do for Your Garden Soil." *Bob Vila*, 6 Apr. 2021, www.bobvila.com/slideshow/the-best-things-you-can-do-for-your-garden-soil-52131.

N-Sky. "Red Spotted Ladybug Eating Aphid in the Wild." *iStock*, www.istockphoto.com/photo/red-spotted-ladybug-eating-aphid-in-the-wild-gm906798426-249888448?clarity=false.

Nyspace. "Farmer's Hands Sowing Seeds on Soil in Organic Garden. Close Up." *iStock*, www.istockphoto.com/photo/farmers-hands-sowing-seeds-on-soil-in-organic-garden-close-up-gm1404668269-456825520?clarity=false.

Our Endangered World. "6 Best Solar Heaters for Greenhouses: Solar Thermal Options." *Our Endangered World*, 1 Dec. 2022, www.ourendangeredworld.com/eco/solar-heater-for-greenhouse.

Planet Natural. "Beneficial Insects for Garden and Greenhouse." *Planet Natural*, 8 Mar. 2018, www.planetnatural.com/pest-problem-solver/beneficial-insects.

"Planning a Square-Foot Garden: Grow More in Less Space." *Almanac.com*, www.almanac.com/planning-square-foot-garden-grow-more-less-space.

"Prevention Is The Best Cure." Natural Solutions, no. 216, InnoVision Health Media, Inc., Oct. 2020, p. 10.

PlazacCameraman. "Sheet of Polythene Laid Loosely Over a Polytunnel Construction Prior..." *iStock*, www.istockphoto.com/photo/polytunnel-under-construction-gm1291647638-386707130?clarity=false.

Schulzie. "Rain Barrel in the Garden." *iStock*, www.istockphoto.com/photo/rain-barrel-in-the-garden-gm522471372-91647995?clarity=false.

Sproutwell Greenhouses. "404 Not Found." *Sproutwell Greenhouses*, sproutwellgreenhouses.com.au/blogs/news/tip-7-greenhouse-pollination.

Square Foot Gardening. "Planting Chart Cheat Sheets." *Square Foot Gardening*, 22 Mar. 2022, squarefootgardening.org/planting-chart-cheat-sheets.

Swett, Lindsey. "How to Determine How Much Water Plants Need: 15 Steps." *wikiHow*, 16 June 2022, www.wikihow.com/Determine-How-Much-Water-Plants-Need.

Technology Exchange Lab. "Native American Three Sisters Gardens." *Technology Exchange Lab*, www.techxlab.org/solutions/old-farmer-s-almanac-native-american-three-sisters-gardens.

Viskova, Veronika. "Conception of Gardening, Healthy Food and Eco Products. The Small..." *iStock*, www.istockphoto.com/photo/small-greenhouse-with-growing-tomatoes-and-cucumbers-in-the-garden-in-summer-gm1328384381-412459138?clarity=false.

Walton, Jane. "Thyme Companion Plants: 10 Best Companion Plants for Thyme." *UnAssaggio*, 4 June 2021, unassaggio.com/thyme-companion-plants.

Ward, Mary. "How to Clean, Maintain, and Store Garden Tools." *Gardening*, 29 Oct. 2021, gardening.org/clean-maintain-and-store-garden-tools.

Waterworth, Kristi. "Common Greenhouse Diseases: Tips for Controlling Disease in a Greenhouse." *Gardening Know How*, 25 Mar. 2021, www.gardeningknowhow.com/special/greenhouses/common-greenhouse-diseases.htm.

Watson, Robin. "Home Greenhouses: Complete Guide With Everything You Need to Know." *GardenBeast*, 27 Feb. 2020, gardenbeast.com/greenhouses-complete-guide.

"When to Transplant Seedlings From Seed Tray." *Greenhouse Today*, 5 Nov. 2020, www.greenhousetoday.com/when-to-transplant-seedlings-from-seed-tray.

Winter Greenhouse. "Fruit Trees." *Winter Greenhouse*, www.wintergreenhouse.com/plant-guides/fruit-trees.

Printed in Great Britain
by Amazon